Run To Save Your Life

Multiple Contributors

Foreword

Runners, real long-distance sorts, are a study in contrasts. They cause their hearts to race for hours, that those hearts may beat slower at rest. Much slower. They make themselves short of breath for hours, that they may enjoy long cleansing breaths and calm at rest. They rise when it is dark and run solo for hours, only to watch a grey or wet or snowy dawn. Yet, they want to share their experiences.

Despite the trope of the solitary long-distance runner, ultramarathon runners have a tradition of sharing meaningful experiences, via essays, race reports, remembrances, poems. Blogs, listservs and social media accounts, are full of runners sharing something they found important. Fellow runners consume these writings: for reconnaissance of a race they intend to do, for the commonality of the ultra-experience, or for making a pleasurable connection.

What we have here is a collection of reports, essays and poetry from many writing runners. They span from detailed reports of iconic races or world-class efforts, essays on runners lost to time, vignettes on brief encounters on the road or trail, to poetry inspired by a thought or moment on the run.

Compiled and edited by the indefatigable Amy Mower*, *Run to Save Your Life* is a collection that "runs" the gamut from lengthy and detailed race reports to simple and poignant haiku. If you are a runner, these writing will "give you that feeling," and you may find yourself with shoes on, heading out the door. If you are a former runner, you just may feel inspired to start anew. If you've never been a runner, you just might feel a stirring in your soul. Something may be calling you to quicken your heartbeat and get out in nature to save your life. Especially in these trying and challenging times.

*For those of you who don't know Amy Mower: she is literally as close to indefatigable as a human gets. She has run over 200 miles in a 48 hour race, over 450 in a 6-day race. She has run one of the world's most famous ultramarathons, the Spartathlon, traversing the roads (and some trail) from Athens to Sparta, over 153 miles. She thinks nothing of getting up at 3:30 to get the morning 20 miler in before work. When she is not running, she is a champion bread baker and knitter of sweaters and hats and mittens and socks for friends. She is a woman endowed with far more than her share of personal energy. *Run to Save Your Life* is her gift to the people and sport she loves and performs with such virtuosity.

Frederick Murolo

Dedication

This book is dedicated to all of you who get up before dawn, who climb mountains and trails, who run in circles and eat M&M's and crackers, who find the deepest of joys in running forever.

Rock on.

Acknowledgements

A compendium of stories and poems cannot happen without the contributions of many people. I am so grateful for my running community for sharing their love of both the sport and of lyrical writing in the form of the works you will find following in this book. I was amazed when I put out the call for submissions by the number of people who wanted to contribute. Thank you, runner writers, for sharing your stories and your lives.

First, huge gratitude to the runners who have spent countless hours with me, sharing stories, pain, joy, tears, sunrises and sunsets. I adore all of you and cannot possible name all who are special to me in some way – but a few require particular call-out. First, to my Runner Girl Katie Smith Stilling – I love you loads. Thank you for sharing dark trails and getting up early with me. To the only person I've been able to truly comfortably run 100 miles with and, for a short time, co-member of the 2 person Unemployed Runners Club – Larry Huffman. To Patrick McHenry who mentored me early on and introduced me to trails and a love of the sport. To Maria ("Nica") Shields, and Dani Seiss – we shared some amazing Sunday Annapolis runs full of poetry, beauty and friendship. Nica taught me the meaning of fierce drive as I watched her on her way to a world age group record, putting more effort into the last mile than I could have dreamed was possible. To my friend Laura Monroe-Duprey for Sundays on the Potomac. To my Connecticut LADS. Super special gratitude for my cousin Rebecca Manion Makas for her wisdom and for always being there. To Deb Ross for her love of shock value which masks her truly wise, gentle and loving badass soul. To Ed Rudman for his unwavering support and Sumartya Sen for sharing my first 100 with me. To the Race Directors and Timers who make this crazy sport possible. To my new Seattle friends Jill Hudson and Steve Brooks for making COVID tolerable.

A special thanks to Fred Murolo who served as editor and

mentor. Fred spent countless hours looking at the little tedious details. Fred, author of "Running Home" has several pieces in this book, and has been a mentor both from a running and a writing perspective.

Thanks to Big Bad Bob Hearn for not only contributing a story, but his awesome Sparthathlon photo for the cover. Bob has been both a running mentor and a friend. His knowledge and scientific study of the sport is mind blowing – plus he's a great guy.

Last but not remotely least, thank you thank you thank you to my amazing family. To my parents Pat and Phil Mower – who taught me the value of hard work to get what you want. To my brother Dave and his wife Cindy for their friendship, support and love. To my daughter Patricia who I love more than life itself and who has taught me the meaning of letting go, and to her husband Cal for being there for her. And to my husband and ultra pedestrian Benjamin (BJ) Timoner – who provided a patient ear and great editing suggestions for the final work.

Contents

RUN TO SAVE YOUR LIFE

RUN TO SAVE YOUR LIFE

Two Old Men Meet On the Road
dallas smith

The vehicle came from behind and slowed alongside to my pace. Then, and only then, I looked over, because I was running in the country and you never know. The dogs run free and their owners tote guns.

But it was Jack Gordon in his Jeep SUV towing his boat.

"Wouldn't you rather go bass fishing?"

The sun was bright. It was a good day to go fishing. I could see he was getting a late start for the lake. So I just laughed and replied politely.

"Well, good luck!"

"Well, that's my offer," he says.

"I understand, but I've got to finish this 12-miler."

I could've jumped right in. Why not? He'd have all the gear I could need.

If you knew anything about bass fishing, you'd know it was good fortune to be invited by Jack. Nobody in these parts knows more about bass fishing than he does. A retired professor, like me, old like me, he has a PhD in engineering and expert knowledge on water quality that gives him insight into fish behavior.

He'd put me on top of fish, tell me what bait to use and how deep to fish to catch a tub full of bass. I knew that well enough. He has his skills, I have mine. I had to decline.

As Jack pulled away I could see there was no one with him in the Jeep. He was running solo, too.

Two grizzled old men in their 70s with well-honed but different skills meet on the road and then go their separate ways. Despite their separate skills each one is learning the same lesson, one all old men know: You go alone now.

Just an Ordinary Run
fred murolo

All:

While we are waiting for Volstate to start tomorrow, I thought I would share yesterday's regular old run. No dragons were slain, nothing special happened.

It rains on and off overnight, but the heavy rains come while I am brushing my teeth. I walk downstairs and put on my shorts and singlet. I grab the Hokas with only 600 miles on them, thinking I might need more traction on wet pavement. The socks are only a little dirty. I pick up a face towel to stick in my shorts so I can wipe my face mid-run. I walk through the house to the kitchen, and the heat and humidity hit me. The rain drums on the kitchen roof. I feed the cats. I have a cup of tea and dawdle for a few minutes waiting for the rain to pass. I come out of the bathroom and it's just drizzling, but I have burned 20 minutes waiting for it to let up.

I put on my cap and head out the door. My timing is good today; it's just a misty drizzle, and I can see a swatch of blue coming over the ridge to the west. I have enough time for a good run, but it's going to be slow. I have the Garmin on and it says 10 something, so I pick it up to get the first mile done in 9:58, and I'm not feeling it. The vapor is rising from the rail-trail pavement; the air is thick. The canal next to the trail is full with last night's rain. I see the old fast-walking guy and he's carrying his umbrella. We exchange good mornings, as always. I see the old slow-walking guy. We also exchange good mornings. On the way back he would say, "Have a nice day," as I waved. But I won't see him on the way back today.

The second mile passes in 9:45; it's still not coming easy. I pass the lock and lock-keeper's house for the old canal at about two-and-a-half miles. Built in the 1820's to transport goods to and from the manufacturing hub of Northampton, the canal was short-lived.

15

The train came and put the canal out of business. Then the world moved on and the rails were torn up for the linear park. I pass the guy with the black dog on a rope leash. He just says, "Morning," as he does every day. Three miles passes, still slow. I head on toward the old swimming hole at the bridge. I see Dennis and his wife's two show dogs (boxers). He's soaked. "The rain didn't cool it off at all," he growls. "Not a bit," I say. He laughs.

I cross into Hamden, pass miles 4 and 5. Still slow, still labored in the thick air. I nod to two more runners. I think about cutting it short on this lousy morning. I pass the street for Aunt Chilada's, the Mexican place. I pass the back of the stone and gravel place and the Italian restaurant. Then there is the back of the dive bar where on an early Sunday run last winter, I saw a chair, a puddle of puke and a pair of women's panties on the edge of the trail. I pass 6 miles.

I'm at 6.5 and about to turn, but a guy is stopping to let me cross West Woods, so I go a little farther. I see a fox cross the trail. I turn for home. Still no mile less than 9:30. I'm thinking a little over 13 and about 2:10.

Mile 7 passes in exactly 9:30 and I'm heading home, so why not push it a little. I'm soaked in the sweat that won't evaporate. Maybe I can shave a minute or two from this run. Mile 8 is 8:45 and that's a lot harder. My shorts are starting to sag with the weight of the sweat. Mile 9. 8:32. I hold the towel in my hand and pull the drawstring tight to keep the shorts up. I push it a little more. Mile 10, 8:18; mile 11, 8:17. Sweat is dripping heavy off my cap. Now I'm thinking 2:01 for 13.1.

At 11.2 or so, I look down at the Garmin and it reads a 7:55 for this mile. I lay on a little more to keep mile 12 in the 7s. It passes in 7:51. Now I'm pushing it back up the hill to get to the half marathon distance in under 2 hours. I just make that and finish with 13.5 in 2:04. I take the cap off and swing it so the water flashes in an arc. I take of the shirt and wring it on the driveway. I groan as I lean on the bannister of the porch steps. I go in and strip down. Everything is drenched.

I save the run on line. Average pace 9:08 according to Strava. Nothing special. Goes in the online running diary under the easy category. Just another summer morning run.

Running To Something Better

amy mower

It's a different sort of dark of late
weighty,
muffled,
bleak
(soul crushing)
just getting out of bed's a win.

The want is hidden deeply
in this time when nothing matters
but this much I know --
in this peril lies promise.

Deserted streets
except for the occasional
(virus spreader)
staggering,
drug crazed,
half dressed,
wrapped in tatters,
no shoes
hacking sniffling
demon in the dark ...

socially distance by swerving 6 feet
fleeing the post-apocalyptic street,
once vibrant,
now closed,
boarded up windows bedecked in paint
the murals implore "Stay Home", "Stay Safe"
some solace that even in this wasteland
there is art to be found.

RUN TO SAVE YOUR LIFE

Heavy dark
Lethal dark
the air ahead is sweeter.
Leaving the carnage
in my dust
I'm running to something better.

Park Closed - Dusk to Dawn

dr. lisa butler

How familiar this road;
every turn and inch, each tree and shrub;
but today, I find no comfort here.
Small leaves clatter in the wake of my heels like
sprinkled bones;
fast breaths echo in my ears,
as if a phantom runner dogs my stride;
the bushes loom dark in shadows, hiding secrets from
the night;
even birds are hushed to catch the whispers.

I run,
my quickened feet pounding away from imagination's
doorstep,
toward the glow that promises a haven.
Even as I flee, the shadows fall
from the bushes like so many snakes
and slink away along the ground
as if they are as afraid of what dawn reveals
as I am of what darkness hides.

The Dark Places

gary cantrell

they know the dark places

i read a list of names this morning.
a list of runners who were strapping it on to duel in the backyard.
as i went down the list,
i saw the names of the seasoned veterans
names that read like gunslingers from the wild west.

not so long ago,
when backyard ultras were rare
i would read the list of names
and think;
"he is a tough guy. i bet he wont give up easy."
"she is very competitive. I bet she is a tough nut to crack."

now you see the names sprinkled in.
hard. tough. leathery gunslingers ...
the ones who know the dark places.
the ones who have crossed the vast desert of endless nights
and gone over the mountains of new sunrises.
the ones for whom the dark places
are as comfortable as the local saloon.

and i know the green ones are watching them.
the efficiency of setting up their base
the placement of their little gear
for transitions that become all too short.
the efficiency of their preparations.
to go to the dark places they already know.

the way they conserve their energy
which will all too soon
be all too limited.
their battle is already half won.

everyone is ready for when it is easy.
these denizens of the dark places
already know what it is like when it is not.

they are ready for the duels.
for that monstrous task of rising
and stepping to the line again
when they can no longer remember how many times it has been.
of chasing a finish line that does not exist.

they know what it is like to see the sun on the horizon
and stop to remember if it is going down,
or coming up.

for now, it is the green ones that laugh
and cover nerves with a facade of confidence.
the gunslingers are quiet.
they survey the field thru narrowed eyes.
their faces a mask.
already
even before the first bell
the mind games begin.

later
when the survivors reach the dark places.
then they will smile.
giving no sign of the pain within.

over the next few days
new names will be added to the list
many will turn away,
when the door to the dark places opens in front of them.
some few will step in
and become legends of their own.
they will chase the unknown finish line.
they will press on,
until all hope is gone.

RUN TO SAVE YOUR LIFE

if they are lucky
(good luck or bad, i could not say)
they will be there until the final two
and fight the ultimate duel ...

for all or nothing.

and write in blood and sweat
the stories that are told and retold
back in camp.
by those who turned away at the door.
when the dark places beckoned.

and at the next backyard
the green ones will be watching them
wondering what they will do.
because they are the ones who know the dark places.
and their battle is already half won.

Light

amy mower

Rhythmic footfalls transform dark into day
pumping legs and beating heart are pistons
drawing lightning from the earth
step upon step
my direct current
forges brilliance--
my private sun.

Fingertips tingle
hair on fire
electric sparks leap from
ground to feet
dark city womb gives birth to stars
a brief (eternal) pause
City lights glitter now;
moonlight brightens clouds
with shimmering joy…
I am, for a moment, blinded.

Ironic that these nighttime hours
are the brightest light of Seattle day

Post run, post joy,
dim drippy gray, or watery sunshine--
shades of pewter streaked with despair
nibbles relentlessly into my joy

Leaden skies
negative pressure
sucks energy like
air from a room.

Spring

karen fennie

I was there the day you were born
Slowly unfolding from the loamy forest floor
Opening your tiny pink fists as the day grew warm
You poked your head through last fall's leaves
And turned your yellow face to the sky, smiling
It feels good, doesn't it?
To be alive again

The Race I Won and Lost
dani seiss

LOST

/lôst,läst/

1. unable to find one's way; not knowing one's whereabouts.

2. denoting something that has been taken away or cannot be recovered.

I lost it.

By both definitions.

Several times, I had massively deviated from my normal, and it had taken me places—some of them marvelous, stark and breathtakingly beautiful—that I would never have experienced had I not been running long on some remote mountain trail. More importantly, it had taken me out of my head; out of the thought traps and ruts that had kept me from seeing the wonder in the day to day, the miraculous, the sublime.

And it had also taken me to where I was now: stumbling around on the summit of Hankey Mountain in the George Washington National Forest in rural Virginia, alone in the dark, sometime between three and four in the morning, my dehydrated, glycogen-deprived brain struggling madly to figure out how in the Hell I had somehow lost my bearings.

Lost my lifeline.

Lost the trail …

Going into this race, The Wild Oak Trail 100, I had silently been a little bit concerned with staying on course. For this low-key, no-cost event that was unapologetic in its descriptions that included "no course markings" and "little aid," the first of a quick laundry list of guidelines was:

1. If you are even the least bit worried or concerned about getting lost, don't come.

But I figured I had time to nail down the forks and crossings of this 28-mile looped trail that boasted nearly 8000 feet of ascent. I had run it once with friends, through the night a few years earlier. And I could run with friends who were planning to run it for training before the event—and during for that matter. I even had friends who had come out and run it through the night completely alone. Why worry? Also, if I got lost in the woods, that wouldn't necessarily be so bad, provided I prepared for such. It wouldn't be the first time. But that's another story.

So I went out a few weeks before the event and ran the loop through the night again with a group of trail-seasoned friends, noted the turns and crossings and landmarks, and then studied carefully every map I could find.

My confidence grew.

I wanted to participate in this event for several reasons, but the main one had to do with setting myself on a path toward better self-sufficiency in running on mountain trails and towards purposes —vague though they were —beyond racing (even if my idea of racing was just against myself and the clock). I felt I wanted to be part of a paradigm shift I'd witnessed in a part of the running community—from racing to running primarily for other aims. I wanted to go beyond finish times and following streamers, to dig deeper to find a more personal challenge in a mountain run, to really understand what it is that makes us push ourselves in such a manner over punishing terrain beyond an arbitrary cutoff. I needed to have a better idea of exactly what I was doing out on those mountain trails and why.

As it stood, I figured I ran to test my limits, to reboot and shake out what I needed and didn't need, both on trails and off, to focus my thoughts, to improve my strength and stamina, both physical and mental, to conjure grit and to really know myself better. And, well, because it is fun! Few things bring me so much joy. But there was something more I was seeking that I had yet to fully understand.

Maybe sometimes you need to get lost to truly find yourself.

After three and-a-half loops into the race, and many adventures running with friends, making new ones and running alone, it felt like a lifetime had passed. Now I was on the last loop, running through the second night, solo this time.

It proved a vastly different experience than the previous loops. Solo at night, after much sleep deprivation, is a game-changer.

When I finished climbing the heart-pounding, slippery-leafed section known as the chin scraper, and finally summited Hankey, the 12th long climb of the run—during which I motivationally told myself I would never ever have to climb it again—it was the wee hours. But I knew that up here on the summit I could get a text through to my husband to let him know I was alive and well. I stepped off the trail and tried to find a spot where I could get off my feet for a moment. I ferreted around a bit and found a rock to sit on, pulled out my phone and texted. He was still awake at 3ish AM and responded, thanking me for getting in touch. I can only imagine the worry I must cause him on these excursions. At least, I know how fretful I would be were the situation reversed. But he understands better than I why I do this, and constantly fed me words of love and encouragement. He even texted while I was out running, not knowing when or if I would get it. Not all spouses are so supportive of runners' endeavors and excursions. I do know how fortunate I am. I am reminded of that consistently. Being in contact with him now was a joy I simply cannot capture in words.

After a few minutes, I packed up and set out to find the trail. But it had somehow disappeared.

"Weird," I thought. I knew I wasn't far off. And then I saw the sign post for it. "Oh yes!" And the descent right there next to it. Though it looked steeper now than I remembered. But this had to be it. I hadn't realized it, but somehow, I had gotten turned around. Such a silly mistake didn't seem possible, but sleeplessness had eaten moth holes in my logic. My prefrontal cortex was all but shut off.

Down, I went…

Down…

Down…

Down…

Down, down, "Damn, this is steep. I remember making good time on this before," down I went. "I must be really tired. But there are the blazes. Maybe this is the old section of trail? And I should be on the new construction that is not blazed?" The trail around Hankey had some new sections created to be more mountain-bike friendly, and these were not blazed.

I stopped about halfway down the mountain. It didn't feel right. I broke out my maps, and found a note about the continuation on the far side of Hankey of the new trail work for the mountain bikers and the lack of blazes on this stretch. It also said the trail continued from the summit to the left of the sign. I believe I had gone to the right. No, I was second guessing. There were blazes. "This has got to be the trail." I kept moving, and ran on the flat when I got to the bottom. Now, I became unsure again. "Shouldn't I be climbing towards some switchbacks?"

I remembered them distinctly. I had just run this loop three times! "Where in the Hell are they now? Well, everything seems to be taking longer on this loop," I reasoned. I stopped and looked around; noticed the constellation Orion, bright in the sky, behind me. "Behind me!" I had seen it the whole way up the Hankey climb. I was facing the wrong direction. "Crap."

Again, I couldn't be sure. I hadn't really been paying close attention to the sky. I could be mistaken. I continued. I wasn't trusting my addled brain. I watched for any sign of landmarks along the trail. There was the sign post for Duncan Hollow which I'd remembered passing on my way up. But did that access the Wild Oak Trail more than once? I couldn't be sure. It was possible. I was about to stop and check the map again when I noticed a tree that looked familiar—as I had stopped to pee behind it before the climb. "Noooo," I thought. I checked, and sure enough, its base was surrounded by wet leaves. It took this whole series of context clues and then the firm proof of that "pee tree" to convince myself of my mistake and get me back on track. "Wow."

I grew rather annoyed with myself then, for making such a silly mistake, particularly since I had been putting so much into navigating. Off I went to climb the last climb—again! Climbing that damned chin scraper again was my penance. Thirteen climbs. This was not your average 100-miler. At the top, I realized it was actually quite hard to find where the trail continued, but at last, I did find it, and was so damned grateful.

Later, I learned I was not the first to make this mistake. Apparently, there had been others—yes, more than one runner — one even with a fresh-minded pacer who knew the trail well. Somehow, this made it a little easier to live with.

The rest of the loop went well and without incident. My feet would get sore sometimes, and then suddenly feel better, which was strange. I ran a great deal of it. It felt easier than fast hiking. My stomach churned for food and I choked down bites of date bars to quell it.

Dawn came on and the forest faded into view, looming large outside my little light bubble, breathtakingly primeval, with giant, near-black, hunter-green columns of trees surrounded by faint, silver-white fingers of light. It grew even lighter, and a faint mist enveloped the mountainside, the large, rugged pieces of time-worn rock growing from it nearly as tall as the trees in places.

A lone bird with a call I couldn't identify awoke and moved about the trees. I had run through here three times now in the past two days, but this was all new and different. This was like seeing Brigadoon, and something about it stole my breath and my heart.

An odd contentedness came over me, as if I had been running this trail for all my life, and now I wasn't in a hurry to leave. But I pressed on with the fresh energy only dawn can bring, bounding down the rocky trail undulations, watching intently for that tell-tale switchback, then that sharp turn with an overlook sign that would soon lead me to the swinging bridge over the river—the singular certainty that I was near the trail head.

At last, I ran to that bridge, but afterwards, took my time and walked for a stretch along the river, it being now light enough to see the cliffs on the far side in the early light. I was nearly done, but now I didn't want to be. I had become part of the trail. Part of these woods. And I realized then with no uncertainly that I had to leave a part of myself here in order to return.

My heart still falling at the experience of the sheer majesty of this place at dawn, I moved out onto the road, crossed it, and ran the last stretch of trail into the camp, finishing as first female.

Still lost. But now in the most beautiful, heartbreaking sense of the word.

Renewal

dr. lisa butler

My Feet
Are learning the trails again
Learning to roll with the rocks
to find footing in the give of earth
and to skip lightly among the scattering of leaves
that foretell the coming of autumn

I am finding again
the unbridled joy released by the stretch
of sinew from bone to bone
in headlong descent
and the satisfaction
of uphill exertion

Waking in the morning
to that familiar ache
like a welcome friend
with whom to savor coffee and a stretch
Falling asleep in conversation
with fantasies about miles in the dark
and watching the sun rise and set
on the same path

I set my feet on that path
toward something
I will know when I arrive
and remember that one belongs in front of the other
Repetitious alternation
Relentless motion
Reclamation of my self

Coming Home
dallas smith

We'd just finished running the race known as Run For Your Mama 5K, a race in honor of Mother's Day which fell on the next day, on Sunday. I was talking with a man from another town, a stranger to me, an older runner near my age. He told me that he was a high school baseball coach. We talked and laughed easily, as runners at a race always do. Suddenly he turned serious, recalling another time, another place.

His face twisted as he relived the moment, telling me how he'd come home from Vietnam, how he reunited with his mom. I averted my gaze for decency. It took his entire athlete's strength to choke back the catch in his throat.

It was a long journey. Toward the end, he'd hitchhiked and finally walked the last stretch, arriving at his mom's home on a cold morning just as she was sitting in the car warming it up to go to work. She didn't know he was anywhere about.

"I dropped ...I just dropped ... the bag ... and went running. I knocked...I knocked on the window." His hand made the knocking motion.

She looked up and recognized him. He described the surprise and joy. The memory was too powerful. His throat caught, his face drew.

"I opened the door ... There was the seat belt ..."

But they got it finally unlatched.

The telling didn't have to be eloquent. The tears, the joy, the happiness—you could see it all in his face, the memory there.

We stood on the grass, two old men reflecting, remembering. He was every mother's son and his mom was every son's mother.

What Doesn't Kill You Makes You Stronger
amy mower

What doesn't kill you makes you stronger and
let me tell you
at 3:30 I am dying
hacking up a lung
legs burning
eyes bleary and
stomach not quite right
no way can I do this thing
not today and
(maybe)
not ever

April 1 and the
forecast says 30 and wind
Great
Cuz that's what I
need on a Monday
when I'm dying

Slide on my tights
my fleece
ease into my
running self
music on
I head out the door
and into the wind

The down is rough
after Saturday's 50
quads are distinctly
pissed

Still
nothing hurts
and my heart is pumping
wind brings tears to my eyes
and I start to find my soul

The thing is
(today)
I couldn't not do this
yesterday's rest
has me almost crazy
and wondering who the hell I am

Legs pumping
lungs burning
The wind whispers its
pre-dawn secrets
into my ears
Out here with the eyes
the hoots
the rustles
We creatures of the night
commune as we
wait for dawn

Almost home
and the sky is brilliant
radiant pink and gold

What doesn't kill you makes you stronger
and
By God
I am mighty.

Great New York 100 Race Report 2016
fred murolo

I ran a couple of 100 milers this summer, but I have not been great on reporting. Here is the first one: the Great New York 100. It took place the weekend of June 18-19 (Father's Day weekend).

One of the many great things about running ultras is experiencing someone else's idea of a cool run. We all pass trails going off into the woods or drive on scenic roads and wonder what it would be like to turn this into an ultra. RDs think it and do it. The GNY 100 is the brain spawn of Phil McCarthy and Trishul Cherns. Think of the sidewalks and bikeways of New York City as a great twisty necklace and the many city parks of jewels on that necklace and you have the Great New York 100. It's kind of amazing.

So I'm walking through Times Square on Friday late afternoon. The place is alive with action. The superheroes and cartoon characters are there. The body paint women are there. The naked cowboy is there. I'm on my way to race check-in, then dinner. I see Phil and Trishul at the check-in. Michael Wardian is checking in. He looks like a rock star. He asks about directions and pacers and says he isn't looking to go crazy fast, just maybe 16 hours or so. He looks like an ultra-god. Tall, strong, incredibly lean. Not crazy fast: about 16 hours. I walk out and think, "I'm glad I saw him; I won't see him in the race." This proves true.

Saturday morning at about 4:30 I'm in Times Square again at the north end near the bleachers. We're gathering for the race. It's quieter overall, but not quiet. There are about 90 runners, plus various crew and family. We have wristbands rather than numbers because this is not a real race; it's a running exposition. No traffic help, no lane closures or anything. Just 90 ultra-souls padding through the city.

We're off at 5, up Broadway and into Central Park. I'm running with Steve. My wife has urged me to stick with Steve for as much of the race as possible because she fears for my safety in the naked city, and Steve is an imposing figure, not someone who would get mugged. And Steve's a good friend, so running with him is a pleasure. We start our tour of parks: Central Park, Morningside Park, Grant's Tomb, Fort Tryon, Inwood. We see Ray K. and talk a bit. A lot of people are moving ahead on this beautiful morning.

At the entrance to Inwood Park we meet my stepdaughter and I run with her for about 20 minutes. This is a treat because we rarely see each other. We arranged it on the fly in the days leading up to the race. Steve moves a bit ahead as Alyssa and I catch up on family and personal news. She says goodbye as we come out of the park and Broadway heads into the Bronx. I joke that she can't cross the bridge and leave her borough.

I catch back up to Steve as we enter the Bronx and Van Cortland Park, the biggest in the City. In many places in this park you might as well be in the woods upstate. I stop to take a few pictures as proof, then move on. The day is warming up, with a forecast in the high 80s to 90. As we go through the Bronx, the sun is still pretty low and there is shade. We pass aid stations with New York ultrarunner volunteers, all friendly and helpful. I'm drinking a lot of water and eating fresh fruit, especially watermelon.

Somewhere in the Bronx we stop at Dunkin Donuts and get iced coffee. We head out to Orchard Beach, then back to the southwest and into the south Bronx past car repair places and warehouses, onto Randall's Island and then up onto the Triborough Bridge and into Queens. Now it's really hot and there is little to no shade. We get another iced coffee and I down a root beer too. We go through the World's Fair Marina aid station and head east through Queens. We see a billboard with the temperature; it says 88.

The afternoon wears on; the sun takes its toll. We get delirious and start speaking in tongues. Steve: This is really hard. I think I'll volunteer next year -- Non ut sibi ministretur sed ut minister. Me: Wha? Later. Me: Work is going to suck on Monday. Steve: Why? Me: Post hoc ergo propter hoc.Steve: Oh. Still later. Moi: Il fait tres chaud aujourdui. Steve: Vraiment. Moi: Je suis fatigue. Steve: Moi aussi. (It might not have happened just this way, but that's how I remember it.)

It is true that through this time, there is little shade and a lot of heat. There is also a lot of random swearing. At one point, I'm using the bathroom in a hotel. It is nice and cool, and I don't want to leave. I remember a measured mile named after someone on a bikeway along the Cross Island Parkway. We run it, but there seems to be no end to the mile. We swear liberally at the mile and its namesake.

All this time, Steve is in touch with Melissa by text. She is going to meet us and pace Steve at some point. That point keeps moving to a lower mile number. Finally, they agree on 50 miles. We meet at the entrance to Alley Pond park somewhere in Queens at about 5:15 pm. Melissa is not beat down by a day in the sun and she's not burdened by 50 miles and she's fun and nice and our spirits lift. We navigate through Queens and eventually turn back toward the west and go past the Unisphere and down toward the 100k aid station. We get there in about 15:50. It's just getting dark and we head on through Queens heading mostly south and onto Cross Bay Boulevard, which will take us down to Rockaway Beach. I'm really hungry and at some point we stop at a Subway just before 10 pm.

I'm getting a blister on the bottom of my foot from the heat and concrete and walking. I stop on a bench outside an American Legion hall somewhere in Queens and take my shoe and sock off and apply some lube that Steve has. It helps a little. We press on.

Rockaway has a small concrete "boardwalk" and then we move west along the main road about a block from the beach. It's just after midnight and we run a bit. There is a group of about 6-8 people who are near us. We get to Jacob Reis park and then take the bridge to Brooklyn. Then we go down to Coney Island and that boardwalk. At the aid station just before the Coney Island Boardwalk, Ray K. is napping. He gets up and goes with the group we are in. The group fragments and we are at the back. It's the middle of the night. We exit the Coney Island Boardwalk and go past the ballpark and back onto the Brooklyn streets. Steve is showing signs of wear. He was a little undertrained for this effort, and the run spurts are taking a toll and they are getting shorter and shorter. He is cocking his head to the side with effort.

At the same time, I am getting a second wind. I'm getting a little itchy. I have told Steve that I really would like to finish by 8 am, because I need a nap and then have to go out to lunch with the family before taking the train back to Connecticut. I'm starting to feel that we are going to finish too late for that. Then we are at the mile 85 aid station and the beginning of a walking path/bike path that curls around the southwest part of Brooklyn under the Verrazano Narrows Bridge for about 5 miles. I start running and I'm with Steve and Melissa and then all of a sudden I'm way ahead of them. I look back and think that I could wait on a bench, but I really feel like running on to the end, so that's what I set out to do. I make peace with leaving my friends and with going it alone and focus my energy to a single point.

It's just me and a steady run pace and this paved pathway and 15 miles to go. I begin to pass people from the old group that had pulled ahead of us. The group had split apart into singles or single runner with pacer. I pass each person with a wave and a "good job" but I am not slowing down or being social. Single point of energy, running to the finish. Finally, I come up on Ray and he asks where the others from my group are. I say, "back there a ways." And I move on. At the end of the path, the course turns up the hill toward 4th Avenue. I make a quick stop at the aid station at the top of the hill and turn on to 4th Ave. back toward Manhattan. I pass a few more people on 4th Ave. and am thinking that I am inside of 10 miles to go and can run it on to the finish. Then nature calls in a way that is not negotiable and the spell is broken. I stop at a Dunkin Donuts and then have to make a second stop at a Starbucks. This sets me back, but in between I keep on running, try to regain the focus.

Then I'm at the last aid station just before the Brooklyn Bridge, and I'm talking to Steel Town Paul. He notes that I took a lot of time between stations and I tell him I had to stop and he tells me that Ray is ahead of me again. I think it would be nice to catch up to Ray and finish with him.

And I have another single goal and I get on the pedestrian entrance to the Brooklyn Bridge and focus to a single point again. Steady running pace all the way to the end. And it's morning and the sun is on the bridge and it's beautiful. There are tourists on the walkway taking photos. And for one second I think it would be nice to take a picture with my phone, but I can't stop. I can't even slow down. And then I'm in Manhattan again down near the courthouses and heading uptown toward Union Square, then Herald Square, then Times Square. Somewhere around 25th Street I see Ray up ahead and I finally catch up to him and we have about 10 blocks left and we run it in. And we finish together in 27:06 something on a beautiful New York Sunday morning.

My father-in-law is at the finish and we walk back uptown to the hotel. Then, after a nap the whole family walks back to Times Square. It's early afternoon and the race is over. I'm in touch with Steve and Melissa and find out Steve finished in 29:12. The family goes out to eat at Carmines and we have huge servings of Italian food. Then we walk back up to the hotel to get our bags and then back down to Grand Central and we're on the train home.

Great race. Great weekend. Thanks, Phil and Trishul. Thanks, Steve and Melissa. Thanks, Ray.

My takeaway: You get a lot of grit in your shoes running 100 miles in the city, some on dirt and trail. It would have been nice to change socks halfway, but I was traveling light—just a spibelt with phone, money and metrocard and a single handheld. No room for extra clothes, no crew or drop bag. The total of my roadside nutrition was three Dunkin Donuts extra-large iced coffees, one root beer, one 6 inch Subway sub and fountain drink, one Starbucks chai tea latte. At the aid stations (which were great), I ate fresh fruit and pb&j quarters and some potatoes and other aid station junk food, filled the handheld and drank some soda. My immediate response to whether I would do it again was no because of the noise. You spend a good amount of the run near heavy traffic, and it's loud. By the time I was halfway home on the train, that had changed to yes. It's really a great race; the daytime road noise is just something you have to deal with.

Lust for Life
kimberly durst

"All human beings are also dream beings. Dreaming ties all mankind together."

- Jack Kerouac

We stand on the balcony and look out into the night, mesmerized by the spread of lights that extends as far as the eye can see. We wait for it to offer its hand, and take from it aggressively, or slip into it passively, or light it on fire when it doesn't smile or say the right words. Humankind wants for immortality rather than conception. The universe, in all of its indifference, just pushes onward without need for trust or disdain; the world only wants for survival. The relationship can be traumatic, but also, in all of its chaos, the relationship can be symbiotic. We have to want for survival, too. Immortality? Immortality we have already, when we dream.

I've consumed a lot of caffeine. In three hours I'll be running down the road in the cold, in the dark, with the night and a stockpile of daydreams to keep me company. People say we do this because we've been afflicted by something, and we've got a deep seated need to either run from it or learn to overcome it by stripping our illusions of perceived physical limitations. I think we run with it, whatever it might be, because when we're in pain we feel the most alive. It's an affirmation of our mortality, and an opportunity to see ourselves for all we are, and have been, and want to be; we dream without pain, but only in the depths of mental and physical anguish do we understand how precious and fleeting our own mortal existence is. And, in that, we become more than dreamers. The tangible and intangible lose their definity. Consciousness is not so easily discernable as we've determined it to be, separate from our surroundings. We become the world. And it lends itself to us, the way any functional part of an entity works to maintain homeostasis.

RUN TO SAVE YOUR LIFE

My feet have seen better days. The ravages of the Last Annual Vol State 500k have been hanging on like an old boyfriend who doesn't know when to stop calling. Nagging aches, toenails that forgot their purpose, an extra 10 pounds that hung around for an after party that never happened: my body retaliated. Though, it did warn me. For more than 250 miles my body shouted belligerently, in every way it knew how, "I'm going to do it." It forced me awake while begging for sleep; and, I'd lament my hungry soul and eat another corndog. The wires were always crossed, but I wanted it, wanted for it, and languished in it. Again and again, I loved the wanting, and it consumed me-- the intrusiveness of people upon my agonized conception, the wanting for physical validation of my passion for the experience. It was there at every corner, in every pained step, every deep gaze at the stars and neon lights and into another dreamer's eyes. I love hard, and then I loved harder. And it hurt.

... and still hurts.

Whatever exists beyond the confines of these walls isn't waiting for me, and I'm not going to wait for it to catch me. We're in this together, tripping over potholes and catching our breath, crawling into the places that make us wonder, wandering in the space between dreamed conception and the conception of reality. We're all dreamers. And we're all here, laughing, languishing, lucid, in love, and lusting for life.

My shoelaces are tied and I'm ready.

Be Still

karen fennie

I will not be discouraged by your perfect indifference
Warming to you as I go
Across the quiet expanse of snow and ice

Where are we headed today?
Down a well-worn path to the past
To uncover and examine again some old wound

Or blazing new trail
Toward a blinding and glittery horizon
With all the unbroken promises and dreams

No, child
Stop with your fretting and questioning and dark and hopeful
imaginings
Be still

Look how the sun dances through the trees
The many species of clouds in the sky
Listen to the wind and the songs of the hemlocks
Observe the tracks of four footed travelers
Who, in their wanderings, worry not where they have been or
where they are going

Can you understand now?
Do you see?

Lay down the maps and the compass and the plans
There is no secret still held or puzzle to reckon

This, right here, right now, is all you really have
And one day, when the struggle and thrashing about cease
You will come to know
It has always been more than enough

Pacing Hardrock
dr. lisa butler

A long time ago, in a mountain town far, far away… I was talked into pacing a man I didn't know for many miles in the dark. Sort of like picking up a hitchhiker except that you KNOW he's nuts and sick and likely to be hallucinating. But the story turned out well and the hitchhiker got to his destination in one piece. So when that hitchhiker turned up again on the entrant's list for Hardrock 100, I agreed to pace, thus verifying my own level of insanity.

The plan was for me to pace a relatively short distance since another friend wanted to pace the majority of the miles. That suited me just fine. The Hardrock course is known for chewing up runners and spitting them out. I guessed (apparently correctly, as evidenced by the stories of a pacer falling off a cliff in the night) that it wasn't much more kind to pacers.

I drove to Silverton the Wednesday before the race to attend the Runner's Potluck in the gazebo at the end of town. Andrea Feucht had done a great job of organizing the potluck and word had gone around to most of the runners who were in town to acclimate. Everyone stood around eating goodies and swapping ultra stories. I met a handful of ultra-folks and caught up with some of those I already knew. It was an impressive crowd to one who knew a few running resumes.

When the runners headed off for the "long briefing," I hung around the park with some ultra-families and their ultra-pooches. It was a beautiful afternoon in the San Juan Mountains and there was nothing better than lounging around in the soft grass and gentle sunshine. It was the calm before the storm.

In the morning, I hunted down my runner and got "the plan." I was to pace from Ouray to Grouse Gulch, a mere 14 miles. No problem. Overnight. No problem. So I set about preparing my pack to properly take care of my runner. Batteries to fit his flashlight, bug-away wipes, an extra hat and gloves, some incredible maps prepared by his other pacer, and all the usual necessities for a mountain run at night. I also made certain to fuel myself properly with ice cream from the local shops and some good meals with friends. I rubbed elbows with some experienced and fast HR100 runners to gather good running ju-ju. A hike up to Ice Lake with a couple of the Ultra Widows and another Mountain Bike Widow (who was sagging her husband on his 2 week solo ride of the entire Colorado Trail) was also on schedule for the day.

When the runners toed the line at 6:00 a.m. for the race start, I was there. I was excited and nervous for all of my friends who were running. When the race started, 125 runners surged up the hill away from the gymnasium, away from the rock they hope to kiss later, and away from any shred of sanity. The morning was perfect with a chill in the air and clear sky. The forecast held clouds but no thunderstorms. The weather promised to be as close to perfect as possible but the course had plenty of treachery of its own. They certainly don't call it "Easy Rock 100."

Throughout the day, I checked the progress of everyone I knew on the computers in the gymnasium. The updates were regular and very well done. Nonetheless, it was frustrating when a runner wasn't on the expected pace and didn't appear on screen as desired. It was easy to hope that the runner was actually on pace and that the intricate system of radio operators and data entry had somehow simply missed updating that runner. Not nearly like the Tour de France with all its camera coverage and highly paid commentators, though this was so much more exciting and important to the crews (not that many weren't following the Tour as well).

Near the appointed time, I drove over to Ouray to await my runner and hang out with other crews doing the same. Some runners came through looking strong, others looked tired or ill. A few were actually sick and took long periods of rest. Many had stories of difficult climbs, the snow glissade off of Virginius Pass, harrowing scree fields, and descents too steep to run. The rest of our crew was anxious. Our runner had been feeling rough at Telluride and had two difficult climbs to make before this aid station. We waited. A few runners dropped. I was nervous about getting my runner through the night but that didn't keep me very warm. And then he arrived, fired up and ready to tackle the next section.

The directors of this race may be very sick indeed, but they are very smart as well. For all the difficulties they build into the course, they plot and plan little ways to keep the runners eating up the torture and liking it. Each possible drop and crew point is at the bottom of a long descent when the runner has had plenty of downhill time to recover. The aid stations are well organized and well stocked with food for every palate, warming stations, and workers who are efficient and trained to kick runners out.

Before I knew it, we were headed out of Ouray for the long uphill climb to Engineers Pass. The course was well marked in this section (no bighorn sheep or marmot had knocked them down like in other sections) with small reflectors. Trouble is, the reflectors can sometimes dangle in the wrong direction and don't pick up the lights. Nonetheless, we found our way rather easily... too easily, as if the forces of the Hardrock were pulling us into the darkness. Unfortunately, the forces didn't pull us uphill and we had to do that part under our own power. I should not forget to say that the race organizers had obviously paid the gravity bill in full and it was on full force! My legs were fresh but the climb was still strenuous. I could only have imagined how it felt to the runners who had already climbed so much over the last 44 miles...but I didn't imagine it because I knew I had to be a little tough to keep my runner on pace.

The trail climbed through the forest, across scree fields, along narrow ledges, above waterfalls. I was grateful for the darkness. Darkness can be very forgiving. It is hard to tell how high the ledge might be or how many difficult steps one has taken. I made certain to keep my light low so that I would illuminate only short stretches of each uphill. It seemed that we had gone forever when we came to a sign, and in the light of my headlamp it said "Engineers Pass 2.9 miles." I hoped that my runner wouldn't shine his light on that sign, but he did and I am not sure if the sound of his groan or his heart sinking was louder. We pressed onward and upward for only a short time longer and suddenly saw a light. Both of us knew this couldn't be the aid station. We hadn't gone that far since the sign. But there it was, complete with kindly workers, bonfire, and cup-a-soup. My runner sat down by the fireside and waved goodbye to me, wishing me a lovely run through the darkness. I confirmed that he wanted marshmallows and Hershey bars and told him I'd run right down and get them for him. In a flash, he was back on his feet and moving uphill.

A short time later, we finally reached timberline. I had been hoping to get there soon as I knew the pass was well above timberline and we couldn't possibly be close as long as we were in the trees. It seems that as we climbed above the tree line we also began climbing out of the darkness. Close to the trees, things were shadowy but the outline of the top of the pass was visible against the sky. And as we climbed closer, the flashlights no longer picked up the course markers. The switchbacks we had used earlier to climb gave way to trail that climbed seemingly straight to the sky and the red flasher at the top of the pass. That flasher was something like the red cloak to the bull and my runner seemed to grow more inspired to challenge that hill. Like a scrawny and unprepared matador, I scrambled in front of him as if to get out of the way, and he charged the hill.

At the top, we also left the warmth of the nighttime air behind. The dawn had a damp chill and clouds shrouded the tops of the mountains. The view was incredible. Light had reached where we were… perhaps it was just our own radiance at being at the top of the climb with a long downhill ahead. The rest of the San Juans were still slumbering in darkness, looking like something out of Lord of the Rings with their black crags and dark clouds. Slowly, the light crept across the mountains, painting them with color, as we made our way down the road to Grouse Gulch.

Grouse Gulch is a lovely little aid station nestled next to what appears to be a mining ghost town. Its abandoned Victorian style homes with no windows and old mining buildings have an eerie beauty. Grouse Gulch aid station is also home to the best grilled cheese sandwiches I've ever tasted. They season them with sleep deprivation and hours of hunger – the best way to make a sandwich! At this point, I left my runner in the capable hands of his next pacer and changed into my crew hat. I was happy to be done pacing but a part of me wished I was still out there on trail with him … perhaps a part of me was.

A friend who paced the same section of trail was left with a burning desire to RUN Hardrock 100. For me, Hardrock seems like a lovely place to pace. But I won't say "Never"... I think I said that once about Marathons... and 50 miles... and 100s...

Climbing

william hafferty

An ode to
switchbacks;
despite man's effort
to plow thru everything.
With straight lines
and grid systems,
and spreadsheets,
And calendar columns
with time rows
And straight roads and square edges...

The humbling and messy
squiggly line
is anything but
directly up the mountain;
forcing change
pivots
bows of inferiority,

along the straight and narrow path
we suspect we ought be on.

Some Climb to get to Terrapin
dani seiss

"Inspiration, move me brightly light the song with sense and color,
hold away despair
More than this I will not ask
faced with mysteries dark and vast
statements just seem vain at last
some rise, some fall, some climb
to get to Terrapin ..."

Hunter/Garcia--Terrapin Station

Though by now I probably shouldn't, I still find it surprising and strange that at this late point in my life I would find such profound meaning imbued in every other line or so of an old song penned by Robert Hunter and Jerry Garcia. Though I could never have been truly called a Deadhead, never worshiped and revered them as some of those fans I had known, I have marveled at that phenomenon that was the Dead. And I have certainly always worshiped at the altar of music's mystery.

I have never found Terrapin a particularly strong or meaningful song. But even at his weakest, Hunter has a poetic way of dragging us through the mythic -- of surreptitiously slipping us a cryptic line or two that suddenly reveals the bigger pattern some decades later when we are doing a bit of soul searching. And it seems for me that at this particular point in my life Hunter had, with his song, come once again to pull the thread.

It is, in fact, both the first song I ever heard the Dead play live, and the first time I had ever heard it. At a particularly low point in my life, a college drop-out ostracized by family, hitting rock-bottom depressive states, and recently displaced to a bad part of Washington, D.C., thrown in with a few scary strangers I hoped at some point to call friends, I was spiraling down into despair and becoming more and more lost. I had come to this Dead show with a guy I was seeing, but had not known for very long. We were separated in the crowd, and I knew not another soul present. The crowd was huge, surprisingly rowdy and a bit frightening. Much like my place in the world, I didn't know where to look to find my seat, where to stand, or how to be.

The music meandered around loosely the way it does with the Dead, the way it does with the song Terrapin Station, without a strong rhythm, without much seeming structure; still the crowd sang and swayed. Then Jerry's guitar refrain peeled through the din, and everyone together screamed the lyric "Terrapin!"

In the focus and intensity of the crowd, I suddenly found that I no longer felt lost, found it but a state of mind, an illusion that fell away with the music, and I realized that I was exactly. where. I. was. supposed. to. be.

It was a solid if fleeting moment, and the recognition powerful. Music has always had a way of doing this for me, of bringing me back to myself, if but briefly, of reminding me of my place in the universe, of lighting the way so that I might not lose my footing on those dark and winding stretches.

Lately, I have been running a lot. In part, in truth, because I have needed to desperately. I have been passing through some great emotional challenges, and it has kept me strong. Also, I have been preparing for two races: in April, my third stab at Boston, and this Saturday, a mountain trail race called the Terrapin Mountain 50k. Surely it is this race that has brought the old song back into my head. That, and it simply happened to coincide with so much else that made the song ring true.

"While you were gone these spaces filled with darkness

The obvious was hidden

With nothing to believe in the compass always points to Terrapin..

Lately, I have been writing a lot. I write of where I place my faith. I try to focus on not what is fleeting, but on that which abides. But everything in this world seems to shift and change with lightning speed, and recently, if I do manage to pull myself out of that ticker tape stream of consciousness if but for a little, perplexed, I find myself standing on the edge of a vastness, naked and alone before the beauty of the universe. And it frightens me.

I know, there are only but a few things that can bring me here.

"and I know we'll be there soon
Terrapin -
I can't figure out
Terrapin -
if it's an end or the beginning
Terrapin...

Not particularly conscious of the approaching race, that old refrain of "Terrapin!" and its message that had so long ago set me back on the path kept sneaking back into my consciousness until, once again, I sensed those mental bees at work, that subconscious stirring that goes on before a big change/challenge, and I awaited that familiar snap! That thunderous clap of the master's hands that suddenly brings in line again the workings of the conscious and subconscious.

Yes, I have been writing. Cautiously, one foot in front of the other, painstakingly trying to figure out how to reach back into that darkness without losing myself in it again, I have been searching for the right balance of elements, for the correct recipe. I read others' words. They all seem to be able to bravely open themselves up and lay it out for all to see. I know that it takes immense courage. I read between the lines for what they don't reveal. I try to feel it out for myself. How much detail? How much of the self do I share? Can others relate to this? How and when should I refrain to protect others? What can I brush over, where must I painstakingly tell all? And how do I remember it in enough detail to write about without dragging myself through the same emotional states? I find myself writing then editing then deleting, then rewriting, and more often than not feeling like I am losing ground; Penelope forever weaving and then tearing out her fresh work on the burial shroud.

But in hopes of what? That I will at last be reunited with some long-lost heroic part of myself returned to give me the strength to say what needs to be said? For the hope of saving myself from the past by recreating it as art, holding it up for all to see? Perhaps. For so long I had been awaiting the return of my instinct, for the return of my strength. It came in running. Running is the fire whose light has scattered the darkness, and with it, I have burned my own burial shroud. But now I must progress further. Now I must find the courage to climb on, to lay it out for all to see in an effort to help others.

> *"Hold away despair...*
> *The obvious was hidden...*
> *In the shadow of the moon, Terrapin station...*

So I will run long again. Up into the mountains where it works the best. Where I will find my strength again. Where I always manage to lose myself. Then find myself.

> *"Some rise, some fall, some climb*
> *to get to Terrapin...*

I make light of it. It is not a race for me. I am slow. I do not compete but with myself. It is just a little run in the mountains. I'm doing it for fun. I'm doing it for joy. I'm doing it because I can. I'm doing it because I have to. I'm doing it because it saves me from myself. I'm doing it because it holds away despair. I'm doing it because running long is what creates that music of my mind that when played over and over lifts me out of the gray streets.

In my training, I sometimes run long from my house to the National Cathedral, its spires beckoning from far in the distance, glowing like the moon in the slanting sunlight, visible from many streets, from many angles.

RUN TO SAVE YOUR LIFE

"Counting stars by candlelight all are dim but one is bright:
the spiral light of Venus rising first and shining best...
From the northwest corner of a brand-new crescent moon...

But it is in the running, in the journey through the dismal streets that I reach its heights.

"Some rise, some fall, some climb
to get to Terrapin...

Running has always been a spiritual journey for me, and I have been climbing in one form or another for years. It is different each time, each place. But it remains a constant in that it immerses me in nature, even in the city, in beauty, in the sacred, in physics, in numbers.

"crickets and cicadas sing a rare and different tune
Terrapin Station
in the shadow of the moon
Terrapin Station
and I know we'll be there soon
Terrapin -

I can't figure out
Terrapin -
if it's an end or the beginning
Terrapin -
but the train's got its brakes on
and the whistle is screaming:
TERRAPIN !

Mountains -- like races -- I was reminded, are all different, and if we listen each has something important, even life-changing, to teach us.

I never seem to do things in a natural order and in my pre-race anxiety, I had arrived once again at that place where I ask myself so many questions for which I thought I already had answers,

"Why? Why am I doing this? Why this 50k now? And why does it worry me so?"

"More than this I will not ask
faced with mysteries dark and vast
statements just seem vain at last
some rise, some fall, some climb
to get to Terrapin...

I wrote about it, attempting to solidify my thoughts, attempting to draw the reason from my subconscious, reminding myself of why I run long trail races, of why I run at all, of what it teaches me, of how it changes me, of how it helps me help others. But the mystery and the anxiety remained.

"While you were gone these spaces filled with darkness
The obvious was hidden

With nothing to believe in the compass always points to Terrapin...

The turning over of the New Year had left me lost. I made solid resolutions, but fumbled in my discipline, felt weak in my resolve. I had somehow lost my footing, felt unprepared for the year to come. Now contemplating my choice in this race, I even pondered, "What is left in this for me? Would this be my last ultra? Have I come to the end of the trail?"

"I can't figure out
Terrapin -
if it's an end or the beginning...

Came at last the fulcrum in the void--race day, gateway. The day moved like a lifetime, slowly at first, quickly at last, and as I traveled round the mountain, pivoted round the moment, I felt the new day's fresh memories bend my old perspective as light though curved glass.

Now the word, that name that is also a mountain, a race, a song, a place, an animal, a lyric "Terrapin" took on new meaning with each fresh memory, each new layer of metaphor, with each newly burned connection of my pattern-finding brain. Among these, there was that familiar imprint, that weird hint I sometimes get when first meeting someone or someplace I later come to know well and for a long time. I would see this mountain again. Some portions of it felt a lot like other races, even like races I had yet to run.

> *"till things we've never seen*
> *will seem familiar...*

The race, the day was but one long, singular moment. There were long stretches with the field thick with many racers, even stretches with fellow racers whom I had met before. Sometimes we ran in conversation, sometimes in silence. At times it felt like one of those weird dreams one has of a family reunion where family and friends present could never coexist in a true timeline. At one point, someone mentioned that we were running part of the notoriously tough Hellgate course, and "Oh!" a light went on in my head and I pondered, "Here is what my hidden brain has in store. Perhaps this will be the year I will run Hellgate. That is why I am running this now. I have already begun prepping for next Winter." And with that thought I realized that in the thought itself I had begun prepping for the challenges the end of the year would bring. Maybe I would attempt the aptly named Hellgate.

> *"Which of you to gain me, tell*
> *will risk uncertain pains of Hell?*
> *I will not forgive you*
> *if you will not take the chance...*

But a year felt like forever, and forever is a long time. I would not commit. Time will tell, I thought.

The terrain shifted, and the group fell apart. I barreled down the mountainside. In the focus and intensity of the running, I suddenly found that I no longer felt lost, found it but a state of mind, an illusion that fell away with the music and cadence of the run, and I realized that I was again exactly. where. I. was. supposed. to. be.

Just after, I found myself alone on the trail, unknowingly approaching the Terrapin summit. I was but following the race streamers, following the path that lead up and up to steeper and steeper climbs until at last, the rugged terrain shifted again, this time from loose rock and gray-brown trunks and dead leaves to a winding brilliant green, mossy way through a dense, twisted wood of emerald rhododendron foliage. They way was so steep now, I pressed my hands hard into my quads, occasionally reaching for trees to pull myself up. Heart pounding, up, and up, I climbed slowly until the trail leveled out a bit, and then I ran along the mountain's crest, peering out now and again at the far reaches of the Blue Ridge and the green/brown patchwork of farmland on both sides below, until the trail ended and at last I found myself standing at the narrow, rocky point that is the Terrapin summit. Here I could see out in nearly every direction. On the edge of this vastness, I felt it again, that feeling that I had had before the run, of standing naked and alone before the beauty of the universe. But now I was no longer frightened. Now, I was here.

And I know, there are only but a few things that can bring me here.

"and I know we'll be there soon
Terrapin

An Empty Chair '94

dr. lisa butler

You once said,
  "you never fully understand someone
  'til you've run a mile in their Nikes."
And I'm not sure if I ever
  understood you.

But we ran stride by stride
  and pulled up chairs
    to tables laden with life's breakfast.
We laughed together
  over sunrises, mountain air,
    weird dreams, and red wine.
We sang so loud once, in the car,
that our spirits are still dancing.

I ran today.
  The colors seemed softer and hushed
          in the fog
And at breakfast, I tried to fill
  the hollow space with biscuits.
I'm still trying to understand it all
and why there is no one filling your shoes
        anymore.

Sisyphe, saxo

adrian gentry

Cap stones five times round.
The sacrifice does dream so.
No. Taps you nitwit.

Post-Race Reflections
steve tuttle

A little reflection a few days after....

When I was a kid, it was baseball, football, basketball and golf. Some running, not much. After high school, football barely existed except for pickup games in a neighbor's backyard on Thanksgiving. I played softball until my early 40's, played in an over 35 basketball league and played in way too many drunken golf scrambles.

But there was never an opportunity to really compete in any of this. I could never be on the same diamond as George Brett, the same court as Larry Bird, the same field as Walter Payton or the same course as Tom Watson. I could watch, admire and be in awe of their abilities but never have the chance to stand side by side and compete.

Since my mid 20's I have been running on and off. I've lost over 50 pounds 8, 9 times and the only way I can do it is to run. On a whim, I signed up for the North Coast 24 in 2013. I hadn't been running, just lots and lots of walking. I stopped after 37 miles. Went home and had the weirdest nightmares and was disabled for about 3 weeks. But it motivated me, so I stepped it up a little and finished my fifth one this past weekend. I've increased my mileage every year.

The North Coast 24 and USATF Championship has given me something all those other sports have not. To be able to stand at the starting line, shoulder to shoulder with some of the greatest runners (athletes) in the world. I might not be able to compete against them but I can compete with them.

This whole group inspires me from top to bottom. My friends get tired of me talking about how damn good you all are and how I'm generally unavailable the first three weeks of September. I age up next year. Hard for me to believe I'll be in the 60-64 age group. I don't feel like I am as old as I am and a few people don't think I look as old as I am (Thank you, thank you, thank you)!

One of the best posts I've read so far was from Diana Martinez. She said she texted her husband right before the race and asked him why she signed up. His reply was something to the effect "It's called living, go make some memories."

Take the chance, see how far you can go, test your physical and mental limits and live life. I'll be signing up for next year as soon as Brian Polen says we can.

I Am a Multi-Day Runner

amy mower

I am a multi-day runner
my power lies in slow
no fleet footed 7 or 8 minute miles for me
those runners pass me by as I
methodically
move forward,
each step a quest
for that perfect pace
that balance between effort
and speed
to find the zone
where I can run forever
or at least
for a very long time.

I am a multi-day runner
though what I do might better
be called "jog"
or maybe "trot"
certainly sometimes

walk

but always
(at least)
moving forward.

Moving along
in my turtle zone
I envy the hares
I picture their thoughts as they zip by me on the trail
"If she works on it a bit
One day she might (just might)
become a real runner."

(though very likely they aren't thinking
of me at all,
(blonde) ponytails swinging,
chattering,
laughing,
cadence in sync)
they are focused on
nailing their next mile

(I am focused on nailing my next 20)

but still
I feel defeated by their easy speed
it looks effortless
if I moved that fast
I'd be showing it
for sure

I am a multi-day runner
I do not zip
I do not dash
I do not win 5K's
what I do are miles
(and miles)
lots of them
I do them in my sleep

I do them sleepless
I do them slow
(and slower)
I do them (almost)
every day.

A perfect run
(now)
is high energy
and
maybe
(somewhere)

in the 10's.

9's? A dream, once a quarter
or maybe on the treadmill
when I'm striving for fast
the occasional 8 and
(once)
a 7:30

A perfect run is
effortless
and strong
and relentlessly
powerfully
steadily
(that's the key)
moving forward
and when I'm done
(sometimes)

I feel like a runner

Mountain Solstice

dr. lisa butler

Summer solstice
magical moments
punctuated by hail
building clouds
driving rain across the ridges

Therapy found
in the early sunrise
and fairie primrose
in forget-me-nots
reminding me of daze on trail

Renewal in the trickling sound
of snowmelt
and the sensation of sweat
melting from the drift of winter
returning to the flow

Breathless moments
in thin air
reactivating the life-breath
gravity grounding
even as we climb toward the sky

Weeding the garden of my spring
pulling up roots
removing the vines that tie me down
and reaching down deep
for what is beyond me at this moment

I walk
I climb
and finally I run

Things I will Not Bring to the Barkley Marathons

adrian gentry

My New Zealand training camp was unsatisfactory.
May I approach the sign-in tent a second time now my
videographer is ready?
My knees are shot and my ankle is not right. But my injured is
other people's peak fitness. So I am here anyway.
I did not expect rain.
My drone pilot can't find the road crossing on 116.
Can I borrow your stove to boil some potatoes?
I don't like fog. It makes me claustrophobic.
Please sign my orange hat.
I did not expect snow.

Runner Girl

amy mower

I see her for the first time at mile 4. Back then when I only did 10, that probably meant about 5:40am, but because it was early spring it was still dark and what I saw first was the light of her headlamp shining like a beacon coming towards me. Even in cool March (though warm compared to this year) she was in a jog bra, which said to me "self-confident". As we passed one another in the dark there was a spark of comradery and it warmed my heart for the next mile. I was new here ... in this town, on these dark lonely trails, and for a moment I had a friend.

I'd see her regularly after that ... pretty much always at that same spot, just before Lee Highway and a mile shy of my turnaround point. We never talked but just did the runner's wave ... slight little upraise of the hand, little nod, saying "we are both intent on what we are doing ... we are comrades in arms."

One morning she spoke... "There is a creepy guy up ahead... take out your headphones and keep your eye out for him."

"Thanks!" I said, and I did as I was told.

In my head I called her Runner Girl and she didn't know it but she was my friend.

One day she was gone. It took a few runs to realize it but day after day I'd hit mile 4 in solitude. I missed her headlamp and the brief daily connection. There were other runners but they were strangers and it wasn't the same.

It was months until I saw her again. It was at a different spot later in the day ... and she was not alone. She was gliding along fast fast fast, cadence in sync with her new companion. I was invisible to Runner Guy but she saw me and waved excitedly. I waved just as excitedly back and was happy for the rest of the run.

I'd see her sporadically after that, always, now, with Runner Guy.

It was, perhaps, a year after our first early morning sighting. I was walking into the supermarket on a Saturday, early afternoon, dressed like a civilian. A woman who I did not know but who seemed somehow familiar approached me and said "Excuse me ... do you run on the W&OD trail early in the morning with a headlamp?"

"Yes!" I said, and I knew exactly what she was going to say when she said:

"It's me! I'm that girl!"

"I call you Runner Girl," I smile, and say "What is your real name?"

Runner Girl, it turns out, is Katie. We exchange numbers (although for almost a year after that she is Katie Runner in my contacts list) and become instant Facebook friends.

She texted me pictures of the chocolate chip cookies she just baked, with the words "nom nom." (I knew we were kindred spirits). She was marrying Runner Guy next month.

That was a year ago. We run together 2-3 times a week now. We saw a scary naked guy on the trail one morning last October. He jumped up out of nowhere and we screamed and ran the fastest mile of that run. My coach says "Katie makes you fast!" (Katie is fast. I have become faster.) She shared her sourdough starter with me, igniting a passion for bread baking that enriches my life immensely. She is who I can pour my soul out to at 4:45. (She is willing to MEET me at 4:45 in the morning!) Several mornings a week she gifts me 10 miles that make my 18 miler shorter and significantly less daunting. She is who I text when I'm about to get my ass handed to me on a platter at a race. I send her pictures of my bread. She sends me pictures of her dog bite. She runs slow with me when I need slow, and fast when I am able to keep up. •

She started out as a beacon of light in the darkness. And amazingly that's what she still is.

Taper Monday

amy mower

Sunday night
taper week
and without the cold comfort
of 4:15am
without the knowledge
of 10 tomorrow
it is with something akin to fear
that I slip under the sheets into
a restless (but long)
sleep
wake up rested
but terrified
and feeling extraordinarily alone
(even more so than the average Monday)
because, now, I am.

I draw my comfort from my coffee
and don't really know who I am until
I pull on my tights
and my shoes

It is only 20 minutes later than usual
but it feels like longer
I test the air
warm but
(very)
windy
back into the house
for another layer

First steps
are bouncy
energetic
easy

stride is wide -
I fly into the wind
and feel the effects
of my relative rest
and embrace the
power
of this run

I am fast,
so (so)
fast
bounding down the hill,
taking on curves,
legs striding,
arms pumping
hit mile 1
and it turns out
I am not so fast
after all

How is it possible to feel this strong
to feel this ready to fly
and be so slow?
Surely the
next mile will be faster?
(it is not)

I ought to just feel gratitude
that it is possible to run
and feel this good
if it weren't for the voice in my head
telling me I have to do better
to make that cut-off
this run would be
close to perfect

There is comfort at least
in one mile in the 10's
and in the knowledge that

RUN TO SAVE YOUR LIFE

I'm running against wind
there is solace that
on this lonely Monday
I've banished the fear
and found myself again
at least for today
I know who I am
and that it is possible
to feel every atom
of your being

I know what it is like
to see inside my body
I know what it is
to tell fear
to go to hell

There's Magic in the Backyard
casey thieverge

This year, seventy runners from seven different countries congregated in the woods of Tennessee in a little town called Short Creek to be part of something special.

You see, this isn't just any ole place in Tennessee. This is Big's. This is Big's farm. This is Big's trail. This is Big's backyard. Big is a special dog. He once rescued a man named Lazarus Lake. If you don't know Big's story, I suggest you read "The Big Dog Diaries".

Big represents everything good about ultra running and the culture of the sport. Actually, Big represents everything that IS good. Every year, on a weekend in October, Big invites his friends, new and old, to come and play on his trail for as long as they can. This year, and for the second year in a row, I was one of the lucky ones to be part of Big's backyard party.

If you are looking for a race report about the details of racing, lap splits, gear, nutrition, etc., you won't find it here. There are and will be plenty of great race reports out there that will cover those topics in abundance. The Big Dog Backyard Ultra is about so much more than that.

Big's is about friends. (Friday night camping in the backyard is buzzing with energy). Big's is about teamwork. (From crews to fellow runners, there is no shortage of helping hands). Big's is about community. (The Cantrells are gracious hosts and they treat all runners like family.) Big's is about harsh rules. (Like the rules in Laz's pre-race speech … you don't want him to clothesline ya!) Big's is about patience. (Having a plan and executing it is key to success.) Big's is about fun. (If you're not having fun, the "jeerleaders" will remind you to smile.) Big's is about grit. (4.17 miles per hour, how hard can it be?) Big's is about the overall experience. (It's not too often you get to "hang with the tall timbers"… thanks Laz.)

But most importantly, Big's is about finding limits.

Out of all the loops I ran over the weekend, it is the one I failed on that I am most proud of. My twenty seventh loop is the one I remember most. About a mile into the trail everything fell apart for me. The remaining morsels of vigor seeped from my body, my leg muscles and tendons seized tightly, and my will to push forward dissipated from my weary mind.

I propped up against a tree, then eventually sulked down to take a seat on the rocky ledge. My race had come to an end and I knew it. Another three plus miles lay ahead of me to get back to the finish line and turn in my timing chip. It was going to be a long, slow walk. For a fleeting moment I contemplated turning around and just walking back towards the start line instead. But the thought of the remaining runners on the trail battling to finish the loop quickly changed my approach.

I wanted to finish the loop. I needed to finish the loop. I knew those last 4.17 miles wouldn't count, but at that time they were more important to me than the hundred and eight plus miles that came before them. They were mine. Alone on the big trail, surrounded by beauty and silence. Trails, hills, trees, fields, sunrise … it couldn't get any better.

I loved that loop, even though I didn't. I was hurting, but I was thankful. I didn't want to take advantage of it. I savored every remaining step of that loop. I was in a bad place and a good place at the same time. I reached my limit (for now).

There's magic in the backyard … and on that day, on that weekend, on Big's trail, I had found it.

Memorial

karen fennie

Your name is sun-warmed
Gold in this late day light
I rest my palm upon the letters and think
It feels like when you touch someone
Blood just beneath the surface
A low fire
Glowing coals
Embers
We miss you

Bird Bone
shamus babcock

This will be my last post about LAVS for a little while, guys. I'm going to need some time to digest everything, my head is a giant spinning orb right now. Plus, this one's gonna be hard to top.

On most of my significant adventures, I try to bring back a token. A physical object I got while I was there that reminds me of the journey and represents the lessons obtained from the trip. A tuft of neon moss from Crystal Mountain, a piece of cheerful change from Leadville, a small nugget of coal from Frozen Head Park. The things are all enshrined in an area of my house known as the Hall of Glorious Objects. I knew the token from this one would be something I picked up off the road and brought home with me. I just had no idea it would be so foul.

Now, you all know I like taking photos of dead animals on the road and posting them up here. I do it to remind us all about the unintended side effects of automotive activity and to just urge a little extra caution for our furry friends. Nobody's natural defenses guard against the concussive blast delivered by a 65 mph Silverado nor the force applied by a tire 8 times your height running you over. Not even the armadillas. That's how you say it down here.

The roads of Tennessee are littered with the remnants of the Lord's fauna and as my journey progressed, the sadness I felt for these creatures was growing each moment, eventually calling me to act. So on day two, just as the nausea caused by the previous day's heroics in projectile vomiting had started to subside, around the time I'd seen my thirty seventh or thirty eighth vulture carcass of the day, I looked down, realized what I had to do, and I took a big gulp.

In the world's truest ever example of "Embrace the Nasty" ever observed at Vol State, I reached down and literally embraced the nasty. First, I dumped the change out of my change baggie into my gum baggie and placed it on the pavement with it open. I then selected a small wing bone, one with the least amount of decaying and decayed soft tissue material I could find, grasped it between my

76

thumb and index finger, and dropped it quickly into the baggie. I took a deep sip of water with my "clean" hand and spit it all over the two tainted fingers of my dirty hand. I had to clean them. That was so gross.

The baggie containing the sacred item was then placed in the bottom of my pack, far below anything I was ever going to use. Just the thought of having that thing and knowing I'd be carrying it for the next 3-8 days gave shivers up my spine. I didn't need to see it again till I was done. I just needed to know it was safe.

I transported this revolting object across the states of Tennessee and Alabama, finally breathing a sigh of relief when I got to Georgia. Soon, I'd be able to get back to my hotel and wash the thing. I couldn't do it during the race because it would violate the principle of what I was doing. Part of what made it real was that the bone was disgusting and potentially dangerous to my health and it had to remain as such till I was done. One of the big lessons I needed to learn on my vision quest was how to vanquish my inherent germophobia. I also knew such a tale would have an impact on the reader. I want them to always think of our furry friends when they're driving. That may be darting under your tire right now!

After I finished and got back to the hotel, I dumped the bird bone in the sink and proceeded to scrub the shit out of it with the bar of soap for a good ten to twelve minutes. Then I washed my hands for another three. Next up was the ninety percent isopropanol bath for two hours, then a smothering of Neosporin plus triple antibiotic cream and a few good sprays off Deep Woods Off before a secondary, bath in the IPA. That's where it is now, where it will remain overnight. When I get home, I'll begin the bleaching cycles.

Now, I know you may all be thinking that I'm a little nuts. Maybe more. But the reason I'm sharing this final piece of my story with you all is because I want to get the message out, if I'm gonna go through the effort of getting the Bird Bone safely into the Hall of Glory, the least you can do is pay a little more attention to God's creatures while you're all out whipping around in your deathmobiles.

And don't hit other people either

A Run With Me...
john ehntholt

With the blue sky only broken up by the brilliant sun illuminating this world, all I see is different shades of white. As I run along this nameless road, all the rawness of the land looks pure under this thick coating of untouched soft snow. The slow moving river to my left moves no more and its dirty water may as well be a hidden rainbow as it lays still and out of sight. Evergreens etched with white tips highlight the other sticks that will push out foliage in mid-May. A large Sycamore comes into view and stands like a guardian between the single lane road that carries me, and the river.

To my right is a rolling field with trees and ledges beyond. I remember it as a cornfield long ago...but there are no clues to suggest that today.

My mind wanders as I stare at the ledges ahead. It would make for a great vantage point to wait and to see what is moving within the area...and today, at this moment in time, that would only be me.

Trail Demons : The Loneliest Stretch of the MMT 100

dani seiss

Usually I am a strong night runner. I crack jokes a lot, especially when others get the crankies and the sleepies. But alone, I cast off the clown mask and let the baggage surface. It was at times cathartic, at times, unpleasant.

But then, it had been my intention.

Inside my head, the night grew darker still. I am not quite sure what others experience as trail demons: maybe just hallucinations. I was having none of these yet. But irrational thoughts and powerful emotions were surfacing and plentiful. I was headed up the climb known as Jawbone onto Kerns Mountain. Oh, Kerns. As I climbed, the wind picked up, and I jumped and started at every unidentifiable noise until I grew a annoyed with my own jumpiness. I thought of my family at home asleep. My husband, my rock, who in my long and weary young life has been the only one who has ever made me feel truly safe. My dog. She is a great trail companion and would be such good company right now. Although, she is even more afraid of the dark than I. She is a smart dog; smart and full of love. I longed for them both.

Oh, Kerns. I had seen it before in the dead of night as well as in the day. But I had never experienced it quite like this. Sleep deprivation can do strange things to the mind. Especially if you let it. I cursed those bloody, big rocks. I cursed the winding trail. I cursed the ceaseless wind. I cursed my lack of agility. I remembered the ridge buried in fog last year; my good friend and pacer, Diane helping me stay on the convoluting trail. Now, as then, I wasn't cold. I wasn't lost. Or at least not in the sense that I was still following the trail. Lost meant something else. My mind unraveled a bit more, and I started to lose my sense of self. I held onto memories as if they were the only thing that separated me from the dark, the rocks. I thought about my mortality. When and how would I go? I thought of my mother dying. A life cut short at fifty one. Fifty one. She had had a rare cancer; had no idea she was even sick. We had climbed mountains together with that cancer inside of her without even knowing she had it -- without even knowing how alarmingly close she was coming to the end of her life.

I cursed the self that had taken her presence for granted. I cursed the self that had dragged her up mountains unforgivingly in that state. Cursed the self that had not valued her life, that had not valued my own. Fifty one. Only five years from where I am now. What was five years from now for me? What did that mean? What is time? I heard again the sound of her death rattle. Her last breath. The sound of her voice. Her singing to me when I was but three years old. The sadness in her voice. Her talking me down from mental cliffs, trying desperately to convince me that life was worth living. Mountains we'd ascended together. And mountains we'd descended, in the dark and in the rain, metaphorically, and actually.

At last, detached, I forgave the self I had cursed, blessed it and let it go.

I remembered the lonely wind spirit my father used to tell me stories of when I was little. It lived off bark and moss, he said, and swept you up with it and carried you away, seeking to cure its loneliness. Its victims always died of starvation and exposure. It remained alone.

I let go then and emptied my head of thoughts and memories. I became the lonely wind spirit. I tripped and cursed aloud. The sound of my voice sounded strange and foreign. It felt like I had been on Kerns forever. How long must I relive these experiences? Feel these feelings? I had never arrived, and I would never leave. I was part of it. What was I? An abstraction? A feedback loop created by my brain? Right now, I was but a memory to others, and this, this thing that had become a part of Kerns. There was only this moment -- reenacted. And continuing. I was Kerns for all eternity.

But I made peace with it. And I followed the streamers placed so lovingly by many golden-hearted friends, away from the past and off Kerns mountain.

The High

dani seiss

It was cold. The ground was so hard. I could feel my spine compress with each step. It was also treacherously icy in some places, so I had to carefully mind those steps. I ran between the river and the cliffs.

One by one the miles return now, each with their own flavor: the glowing ice flows from the rocky cliffs at mile three, the smell of the winter air sharp with wood smoke around mile 12, the daydreaming of warm goats milk with rum and honey at about mile 15 or 16.

I was in a unfamiliar state. I kept thinking about what I would write when I returned -- little tidbits that would best capture it in order to share it with others. But it seems I did not write much when I returned. I don't recall why.

I do remember it well, though, this entire run, even now; that sense of oneness, that now familiar opening up to all of existence, as if at some point the boundaries of where the "I" ends and where the "All else" begins fall away completely. And it came on suddenly, its onset as abrupt as stepping cleanly and squarely off a cliff into the thin, winter air.

Only to discover you have the gift of flight.

More than this, it was as if time itself had stopped. The seconds lasted a blissful eternity. More like there was no time, and no line between the dead and the living. There was this thickness to space and a hum to it all -- that beautiful drone of existence. The air seemed as solid as the trees; as myself. And yet I floated along the ground a ghost -- an invisible cord stretched from my solar plexus, pulling me along to some unseen point on the horizon.

Running Along the River
karen fennie

There is the sun today
Jumping out of the sky like a big surprise
So everyone smiles as they pass, happy for this shiny gift
The ice-clad river has heaved in spots and water races and dodges and
disappears and reappears
Skinny branch shadows painted on snow
And my own form running beside and then ahead of me down the winding path
Oh, there you are, I think to myself
How I've missed you
Welcome back
Keep on going
Never stop
Breathe

The Dog Whisperer
bob lantz

After watching a number of Cesar Millan's "The Dog Whisperer" programs on handling unruly dogs, I was on a 26 mile training run along a busy state highway in rural PA during the peak gas drilling rush, with an abundance of truck traffic. The berm was 3 feet or so, enough to run on, but kind of tight. While motoring past farm house after farm house enjoying the beautiful day and great run I was having, I approached one with a little fluffy dog with a really big attitude that was freely demonstrating to me that it would be his pleasure to ruin my run, right then and there. Having run past many dogs of various sizes and temperaments for years, I would normally stop, face the dog, and firmly tell him, "NO!" while stomping my foot, or something similar. I had never been bitten while running, so it had worked quite well for me. Well, this little pooch was totally unaffected by my overtures, and instead became the aggressor even more.

As I said, the road was busy with truck traffic, so withdrawing across the road was not an option. Each time I would lean toward him, he'd get closer to me and become more aggressive. Suddenly Cesar's instructions came back to me: "ignore them and they will relax," so contrary to everything in me that was saying ATTACK, I began to relax and gave it my best effort to ignore the violently barking little dog a foot away from my leg, (as the trucks whizzed by me from behind). To my surprise, the dog almost instantly stopped barking and turned away from me and headed back to his house. Inside I thought, "wow that Cesar stuff really works," and I headed on past the house much amazed. I got no further than twenty strides down the road when I heard that familiar yip coming closer from behind. In an instant I considered trying a Cesar 2.0 on Fido, then decided a short sprint was in order and headed on down the road to the ever fading sound of Brutus, the badass. I would save my dog whisperer lessons for another day.

The Practically Perfect Run

amy mower

I generally know if a run is going to be good within about a minute of starting out. This morning's route was Murphy Hill. I didn't do a specific speed workout yesterday for my short 5 miler, so I thought getting a brutal hill in would be this week's speed focus. I also had a feeling that today might be my best ever Murphy Hill climb.

The temperature was perfect. Truly perfect – low 50's, gentle breeze, sun not up enough to be hot – just up enough to turn the sky into a sunrise portrait of pale blues, purples and wispy clouds, with some haze here and there. I have been waiting all year for running weather like this, paying my dues during those 5 degree dark days. I was wearing my relatively new shoes paired with a new style of insert, and I was pleased that my feet felt supported, cushioned and that nothing hurt.

In fact, nothing hurt anywhere. This has actually been happening more and more often as I continue to improve my base. When I just go out there and put in the miles at the pace my body wants to go (rather than the pace my brain wants to go), often everything feels good, easy, smooth and natural.

I am starting to accept (or trying to accept) that if I go at the pace my body wants to go, I will almost invariably be disappointed with the time it takes to do my first mile. That first mile is a bit hilly, and although at one point in time when I tried to do every run as fast as I could take it, I would manage it in 9:30, it pretty typically takes me 10 plus these days, as I allow that first mile to be a warmup. Today was 10:25. A tiny little voice in my brain whispered disappointment but I waved it away, happy with how limber and strong my legs felt, and reveling in the astounding beauty of the morning.

The next mile was 9:52, which eased the voices in my brain

a bit. Still feeling good. Mile 3 was 10:10 – that one is a bit hilly too, so all in all, the voices were not overly loud about pace, and they let me focus on feel.

Murphy Hill starts right after mile 3 – it is a 600 foot (or so) climb, in the space of 1.6 miles. Sort of a series of steep rollers. It is my favorite "go to" hill. The first mile of the climb has been known to take me 13 minutes. The way I've been approaching hills has been to take the hill at the same effort as the rest of my run – not at the same pace. Lately this has been just a constant focus on "how does my body feel RIGHT NOW, and what adjustment do I need to make"? Generally by doing that I have a strong climb.

Today's climb was perfect. Every step felt right, and, more importantly, every step felt strong. I could feel my glutes, which I've been working on, propelling me up the hill. I was thrilled when I saw that first Murphy Hill mile took me 11:18. Killing it, and feeling great. One of the best things about today's climb was that it was strong and steady and it felt awesome. Sometimes it is just killer hard – my breathing is rough, and it requires extraordinary mental fortitude to just keep taking the little steps up the hill. That's good training in itself – but I love it when I feel fantastic.

The last section of the hill gets pretty steep and just requires little quick steps, as slow as necessary to get to the top. That section usually feels pretty rough. Today – well, today it felt just fine!

I got to the top and stopped for just a moment to let cars pass and to enjoy the view. And started on the down.

Although it would seem that the down would usually be great, that isn't always the case. I'm not a strong downhill runner – I think I tend to brake a bit, and I'm never quite sure what my stride should be. My approach lately has been to try to lengthen my stride, relax, and let gravity do its thing without me getting in the way. Today it felt kind of like flying. My first full downhill mile clocked in at 9:17 and my next one was pretty close to that. As I concluded the real downhill portion, I caught a glimpse out of the corner of my eye of brown. I quickly registered it as a doe and her very very new, tiny, spotted fawn, nestled down beside her, to the left of me in a meadow. I stopped and reached for my phone to take a picture – but alas, the fawn was gone and the doe started wander away. Damn. I really would have liked that picture. But at least I had the gift of seeing that perfect moment.

As I started to run again, I was thinking to myself, "there is nothing about this run that isn't perfect." About a mile later, I spotted another doe and fawn together in a meadow and realized again how grateful I was for this perfect run.

It wasn't until I was about 3/10 of a mile away from home that anything happened to mar the beauty. There, off to the side of the road, I saw another beautiful spring animal baby – a fox – lying lifeless, killed by one of those awful road monsters, who so often seem like they are aiming their headlights and tires at me. My heart broke just a little bit, and I finished the run on a more somber note.

So, not a perfect run after all.

Running is my Church

karen fennie

In autumn my cathedral has stained glass windows
God has been busy with his palette of oak, ash and sassafras
'Have faith' he tells them
And they slowly sacrifice their solemn beauty

My alter is crowded with curling, crumbling leaves
Swirling..wondering..whispering..
Do you believe?

Black branches bend, to be baptized with the rain
A tender veil of mist anointing holy water ponds
Murmuring, muffled voices
I move on

The priest has passed here too
Swinging his censer of wood smoke and sweet decay
I bow my head, breathe in deep
Filled with wonder on this day

I leave the sacristy now
The sacred vessels
The scaring bells
Hymnal closed
Choir quieted
I go in peace

Suicide Bridge

shamus babcock

Well...it finally happened, Folks!! After all these years of running back and forth over the "Suicide Bridge" I finally encountered my first jumper today.

The actual name of the bridge is the Victory Bridge and it was finished in 2005 and it's 110 feet off the surface of the Raritan River below. This is the time of year that people tend to jump over, call it the holiday blues or whatever, but we are smack in the middle of jumping season. If more than 2 go over in a year, the Perth Amboy cops shut down the sidewalk to pedestrian traffic till Spring and it really messes up my training run and screws with me spiritually.

So on today's run, as I approached Pillar # 6, which is right near the apex, or basically where the red crane barge is sitting in the photo, I saw a car parked on the southbound side with the hazard lights on. My first inclination was a stranded motorist, people break down here all the time, and I even saw a lady pull over once to beat her kids so a parked car is normally no cause for concern. But I saw this hobolooking dude wandering around on the sidewalk and I thought, "Uh-Oh."

As I approached, he said, "Hey Buddy, can you give me a hand getting my leg over the rail?"

I said, "Why, are you trying to jump?"

He said, "Yeah, my life is fucked, I got no money."

I said, "Not my problem, but there's no way you're jumping with me here, I won't help you with that."

He said, "I got no money, I don't want to live" and he made a break for the rail.

I tried to jump in front of him but he beat me there and my

bargaining instincts kicked in. I said, "I'll give you all my money ($5 bill in my pocket) and everything else I have (my chap stick, my tums, and all my clothes and my shoes) if you get back in your car and drive back down."

He said, "I don't need 5 bucks I need REAL money" and then he grabbed the rail and looked over, ignoring that I also offered him my clothes and my beloved trail glove shoes.

He said, "It looks pretty far."

I said, "It's only 110 feet. Everyone that jumps off lives." (A lie). "The water is calm, you'll just hit the surface and pass out then you'll drift to the shore and when the cops pick you up, they'll be pissed and they'll arrest you." I said, "Then they'll take you to Raritan Bay and the ER guys will have to pump the nasty river water out of your lungs and they got more important shit to do ... and when you wake up, the first thing you'll see is me and I'm gonna punch you right in the face for jumping when I told you not to." I had no idea what I was doing so I just kept talking in a very authoritative tone and kept pointing, first at him, then at his car.

Just as I was running out of crazy shit to say, just before I started begging, he took a step away from the rail toward his car. This was my moment to act. I jumped in between him and the rail and I said, "OK, now you have to get back in the car and drive down because you can't jump with me standing here."

He said, "Oh yeah, who the fuck are you?" I said, "I'm the Parakeet of Protection and NOBODY jumps on my watch." Now, I was yelling loud and my finger was about 2 inches from his face.

Maybe it was my threat, maybe his rational mind kicked in, or maybe he just remembered a hidden stash of $ somewhere, but something changed after that and I saw his shoulders droop and he took a VERY deep breath and he took two steps away from the rail and toward his car. He wasn't going to jump and it was time to make good on my promise. I took Abe Lincoln out of my pocket and handed him my chap stick and tums and started taking off my shirt.

Luckily, he decided not to hold me to my promise and he got in his car and turned off the hazards and started driving down.

I thanked him profusely for that. I would not have a suicide on my conscience and I would not need to run the remaining 5.2 miles home butt naked in the cold rain. I ran after his car to make sure that he made it all the way down to the Rte. 9 circle. I had no way of knowing if he'd go back up there but at least I made him think twice next time.

The whole episode only took about 1 minute 45 seconds. know because that's how long my pace dropped to 0 on my GPS. I couldn't believe it. I knew that one day I was very likely to see a jumper since people go over all the time during this time of year. I used to always play it out in my mind, "What would I do if I ran into a jumper?" Well, now I know.

So to all you Victory Bridge jumpers out there .. listen up!!! The Parakeet of Protection will be patrolling that bridge and if I see you up there acting a fool, you better get down, or else I will talk and talk and talk and wear you out, so by the time I'm done, you'll be happy to go back to getting your life back together.

Summer's Dear John

karen fennie

It's time this ended but I will try to be gentle
A few leaves loosened from their anchors
Tumbling down slowly
Finding rest at your feet

Flowers dimmed, sweet smells fading
Peepers no longer call as often in the night
Soon, no calls at all

Most birds will go too
Though some will remain
Dressed in extra feathers and you in your fleece

That warm embrace as you walk through the door
Is no longer mine to give
Please trust me
You deserve better

A gradual tilting away from the sun
At first you'll hardly notice
Until mornings bring chill and you consider turning on the heat

Sorry for stealing light from your days
But only a few minutes at a time
Will you ever forgive me

Everything will stop
Except for time
Which is the only thing that will put distance between you and
what I've done

The Shadow
brian burk

After some hard fought miles I am finally running alone. The sound of the starter's gun is still ringing in my ears and the race has really just begun. All the work, all the missed social engagements, and all those lonely hours on the road are paying off. Battling two would-be challengers for the better part of the race, I am finally in the lead of my home town race, the Brownstown 5k. This race is just like any other run-of-the-mill 5k, but to me, it is unlike any other. At this race last year, I failed. My body let me down. I burned out with the intensity of a solar flare. And this is the race I always wanted to win. Today not only am I now in the lead, but I am also pulling away. At the two mile marker, the majority of the pack was left behind and by two and a half miles I have finally separated myself from my two lone rivals. Out in front, the open road is my only companion.

I have never noticed how quiet racing could be. Normally in the middle of the pack, there's always noise. There are always distractions. The sound of breathing surrounds you. The rhythmic sound of countless pairs of running shoes impacting and gripping the pavement runs along with you. And the nervous chatter as competitors talk amongst themselves encircles you. But up front, alone, and in the lead it's quiet. The only sounds are those of my lungs filling with oxygen and exhaling. The sound of my shoes hitting the running surface and propelling me forward. And, lastly, the absence of sound as my inner voice encourages me. Compared to being sandwiched in the middle of the field, it's so peaceful running in the lead.

Running up front is different than running in the middle of the pack. Up front you set the tempo. If you're trying to win the race as I am today, you set a pace just a bit faster than everyone else. Leading the race means you get to see everything first, guiding the field behind you along the course. Running with the lead also means you have to make sure you follow all the correct twists and turns along the race course. Whereas in the pack you can safely play "follow the leader," up front you have to motivate yourself, push yourself and challenge yourself when there's no one in front for you to chase. And today at this point in the race, the field is far enough behind me that no one is pushing from behind.

But what is THAT? As I glance down to monitor my footfall a shadow appears at my feet. At first, it catches me off guard. Is it a tree, or an animal, some kind of creature approaching me from behind? After further study, the shape of this intruder registers in my brain. The shadow is the head of an approaching competitor running me down from behind. All my senses heighten, the hair on the back of my neck stands up, and my skin becomes electric. My sense of hearing picks up on a sound, the soft cadence of someone approaching from behind. My heart rate quickens, and my nerves are rattled. I look down once again and now even clearer, projected from behind, is the looming silhouette of a runner. And this stranger is growing larger.

Now I am sure that the shadow, the evil figure attempting to steal my victory, is running at a pace that will surely overtake me. My brain fires off signals that call for an accelerated heart rate and over-juiced adrenaline to kick it up to a higher gear. My stride reaches out, my leg turnover quickens and the road beneath me speeds by ever faster. And yet the dark threat continues to loom and grows even larger. Now I can clearly see the shadow of the head and shoulders of the silent figure behind me. My flight or fight instincts kick in and now, without even transmitting the thoughts, my arm swing widens and my legs drive forward. I pass a sign telling me I have less than two-tenths of a mile left of this 5k. I vow that I will not let this menace who lives in the dark, who steals from behind, creep up and capture my day.

My eyes are fixed on the prize. Like a young boy hiding his head under the covers hoping that the monster just goes away; if I stop looking maybe the shadow will go away. But will-power fails and curiosity forces me to look. In horror, I see nearly a complete torso. In fear and panic, I lean forward attempting to pull away from the ghost behind me. My foot strike quickens more. My heart is pounding. My lungs are on fire. I've got nothing left to give and the shadow grows larger still. Only 50 yards to go, and I'm in a dead sprint, my brain lost, my body maxed out. almost home yet the pursuer gaining an advantage with every effort I give to counter his attack. The finisher's tape is just ahead, ten yards then five yards. I'm doing everything to pull ahead to keep the hunter at bay … and with a last push to the finish, I come home the winner.

I'm spent. I'm done. I've given everything I have and I've finished. The race is mine. I have won. Yet I wonder who nearly caught me. As I stumble down the finishers chute collapsing into the arms of a volunteer, I ask, "who came in second?"

With a mystified stare the young girl tells me, "No one, you've won the race and left the field in the dust."

"But who was behind me, who was I fighting off? WHO?" I ask, "came in second?"

The girl, a bit confused, tells me again, "Sir, no one. Second place has not finished yet."

"But I saw his shadow. I saw a shadow of an approaching runner coming from behind. I fought him off for nearly half a mile. Where did that runner go?"

The young volunteer looks at me, and smiles. "Sir, that shadow was you."

Tonight

karen fennie

The run begins tonight as the snow begins
Fairy dust
Confetti
Glitter
The world is mine alone on nights like these
My secret cold treasure
No one knows the salted paths
The silence
The shape of God's face in the shattering sky

Umstead 2019
fred murolo

Steve starts the crap talking early. He can't help himself. Early, like last fall. He is going to lap me. And the laps are 12.5 miles, so he is going to beat me by three plus hours. He has this way of tapping into my self-doubt and imposter syndrome at the same time he playfully talks trash. He's a good friend.

And it happened once; he lapped me in 2015. So, I have to be aware of it. Never mind that I must have lapped him in 2016 and thought nothing of it in the moment. When your friend is 6'6" and 300 pounds., if you lap him, nobody cares. If he laps you, he has bragging rights.

The talk continues on our daily messenger group. Steve thinks he's funny, thinks he's a real character. Should be in a novel or something. If you ask him, he will tell you Rufus is the greatest character in any novel anywhere.

I laugh it off, but something gets under my skin. Around November, I run a nice Sunday 20 miler with super-runner Amy, who is up visiting from DC, and she asks what my favorite 100s are. I mention Umstead and she says she might try it, hears it's hard to get in (it is). I casually invite her to pace me to get the flavor of the race.

I have never had a real pacer in a race, someone who is designated and drives down just to pace you and will stay with you for 50 miles, like you need hand-holding or something. I'm usually the guy toiling alone at night singing to myself.

The months go by. Training is lackluster. I fret about the pacing thing, how it will go. Will it be the most boring night of Amy's life? It will be slow. She's a race-winning, super-runner. I'm just an old guy trying (and often failing) to hang on to the mid-pack.

RUN TO SAVE YOUR LIFE

My training the last year has been nothing special. I have two (for me) big mileage years over 5,000 miles and then back off to 4,450 in 2018. And even that seems harder, and I am sorer and less rested after a long effort. I start 2019 with some resolve but have to back off in February, because I am just feeling overdone. Then in March I feel that good feeling of gently ascending fitness, but it promises nothing for Umstead, except that I will be able to finish.

My race logistics are not the best: my two kids in high school are both in the school play on Umstead weekend. I am at opening night on Thursday (the play is great), and I start driving south at 10:45 pm. I take a nap at a rest area in Maryland at 2:05 and another nap in Virginia in the early morning. I arrive in Raleigh by 12:00 and drive into the park. I pick up my number and go to my cabin. I started staying in a cabin last year when my family could no longer accompany me to the race. The downside is that they are primitive: no electricity or heat. The upside is that they are right on site. You drive in on Friday and don't have to use the car again until Sunday.

I go for a short run in the park. It is raining as it often does the day before the race. I go to the pasta dinner on site and see many old friends from my 12 previous years at Umstead. I go to bed early (no electricity).

I wake up at about 4:50, put on my running clothes and carry a small cooler and plastic bag of clothes to the front of the race headquarters cabin. There is a buzz in the air as I enter. I grab some breakfast and talk to friends. Steve and Melissa, Bill, dressed like a pirate, Mary, Tammy, Juli, Mike, Ray. Many others. I toy with the idea of actually starting near the front, but find myself on the cabin porch as the clock winds down talking to Steve and Melissa and Mary and then we are off in the pre-dawn gloom. At about mile 2, I move ahead of Steve and Melissa and carry a gentle run over the few little rises, down cemetery hill and all the way to the serpentine downhill and first big bridge. I run alone at my own pace and the cool morning feels good, if a little humid. I finish the first lap in about 2:32.

It is light now and I do the second lap in about 2:40. I run some of it with Mike, who is headed for his 19th Umstead finish. (He's done more than 100 100s.) It is already feeling a little harder. Somewhere in the third lap, I tell Mike, I'm not feeling a sub-24. He tells me it is too early to say that.

The third lap takes a little over 3 hours. Amy is there near the end and I stop for a few minutes and we talk. I meet her husband, BJ, who has driven down with her. I take off on the 4th lap and slow even more. By the time I get in, the clock is at about 11:35. That is a slow lap. But it is my 100th Umstead lap, so I am feeling good about that.

Amy is ready to start running with me. We amble off and discuss logistics. She will be more companion than coach but is explicitly allowed to push me if she wants to. When she is bored at our snail's pace, she begins to suggest running spurts based on topography and flora. Run this downhill. Run to that big tree. I show her the walking parts and running parts. She is very indulgent as I am not burning up the course.

Lap 6 is more of the same. Steve comes up on us at about the 9 mile mark of the lap. I speed ahead, not letting him pass. But he catches up near the end of the loop. He has a walking pace that I cannot match. And so it comes to pass that after about 20 hours of racing, Steve and Bill and I end up finishing lap 6 at the same time.

As we are coming in, Steve announces—too loud—that he is in a low energy funk and will need to stop and eat. He runs right through as I expect and tries to put as much mileage on Billy and me as he can. I do eat and drink something and end up a mile behind Steve at the airport spur. I just shuffle along and try to make up ground. Bill, in usual fashion effortlessly dances right past me talking to some friend pacing him. I am not feeling great, but I am determined to close up the distance to Steve.

Then things change.

We come up on a big guy, John, walking alone with a

sleeveless top. He is moving too slow to feel warm, dressed like that. It is his first 100. He is in the DNF zone. Mile 79, underdressed and cold, trudging to aid station #2 where he might drop. We decide to help. We urge him on and walk with him to the aid station where he has a drop bag. We get him to put on warmer clothes and stay with us back to the start-finish. He now has the look of a finisher. When you get to the end of lap 7, you can do it.

We invite John to stay with us if he feels up to it, but it is now the final lap and I want to move faster. John drops back, but he will finish. Coming back from the airport spur, it is full morning, and I inform Amy that I am finally feeling it coming. I am going to start running and finish strong, notwithstanding all the slow and slower walking. Billy, who was sitting at the start-finish as we moved through, passes us talking and walking fast, head forward, elbows out, that distinctive style. I won't see him again. I run down cemetery and run hard down the serpentine hill. We throw in some short runs coming up the hill at the garden spot and then run all the way from the water stop down to AS #2. From there it is 5.5 miles to home. I am pushing it as hard as I can go. On the downhill near mile 9 on the loop we catch Steve who is running nice and easy, looking good. I invite him to run it in with us. He says he will catch up to us on the uphill. I bomb the last section of downhill, carrying it across the narrow bridge, and Amy says, "No, he won't." She's a little competitive. I guess I am a little too sometimes. We walk fast up the hill to the turn and then bomb down powerlines for all we're worth, across the bridge and partway up the big hill. From there we run whenever I can do it. Finally, from the top of cemetery, we run it in.

A mediocre effort overall, but nice to finish and finish fast. 27:45, Umstead number 13. Billy is about 35 minutes ahead. It's his 15th or 16th finish. Steve about 30 minutes behind, finishing his 6th Umstead.

***

I had a great time running with Amy. We have a natural bond; we love higher mileage training. Even though I have been on the downside of the training wave the last year, I love the feeling of really putting my shoulder into the training and feeling the exquisite soreness brought on by big miles. Amy carries that on, and I love and respect that ethic in her. I'm sure I moved too slow for her, but I thoroughly enjoyed what amounted to a 16-hour, all-night visit.

It was nice weather this year and I should have been faster, but I'd be lying if I said it wasn't getting a little harder now that I'm 62. I'm not done yet, but I'm not running times I did even two years ago. That said, I'm not giving in yet.

Next stop: the fair.

My Running Shoes

mary ann clute

My running shoes take me
Out to nature
Where I see new growth and rebirth
Poking through dead grasses

My running shoes bring me social distance
From all but the red-tailed hawk, the red-winged blackbird
And the garter snake sunning in the dirt.

My running shoes
Create a rhythm
Steady and slow
That calms the beat of my heart

My running shoes pull me into
The March gusts of wind
That re-inflate my lungs
And deepen my breath

My running shoes take me
Where I can run my hands over tree bark and
Sun warmed rocks
And touch my face without fear

My running shoes eventually bring me
Back to the official infection count
Back to the mortality rates
Back to the dire predictions.

But my running shoes allow me to
Escape the daily drama
of COVID-19.

So, if I die in this crazy pandemic
Please cremate me
In my pair of Brooks Ghosts
Embedded with dirt and particles of runs
That helped me escape grim reality.

Rainy Run
karen fennie

Logs slick and shiny line the trail
Trees shout yellow gold, yellow gold, yellow gold
Murmur red
Then orange
Black pavement canvas for the leafy collage
Rain slides off the bill of my cap
A wild party ensues across the surface of the lake
I could have watched from my window
Ever the wallflower
But oh, what I would have missed

Baby Bird

amy mower

Defenseless without my miles
easy prey to the seepage of
emotional carnage,
flightless and
afraid
I am a baby bird

With vulnerability comes
wonder and
freedom
(as long as I
can escape this nest).
This haven is
also a prison

There is a fine line between
flying
and falling
(or flying too close to the sun)

One must navigate these skies with finesse.

Full Wolf Moon

karen fennie

You woke me up
Sliding through the window like you did
Casting dancing trees upon dark walls
Pretending to be some kind of night time sun
I had no choice being pulled to the window as I was
You must have wanted me to see your big round face

And all those stars
The drifting snow and disappearing hoof prints
The emptiness and silence
And now, you expect me to sleep
Or is it dream?

From Miler to Ultra Marathoner
george sanders

As ultra-runners, we all have different stories on how we got to where we are today. This is my story.

What led me to even consider this type of distance at all was my background in middle distance running … my favorite race distances are 800m to 5k. In some ways I can trace the origins all the way back to 1970 when I ran my first marathon. I let peer pressure coerce me into entering Boston the last year you could do so without a qualifying time. (I thought it would be my only opportunity to run Boston)! Since then I've run 15 more marathons over the years, but the marathon distance has never been a favorite and I kept drifting back to the middle distance races.

Fast forward several decades. Throughout my 50s I focused almost entirely on the short races and would, only once or twice a year as part of a large group from my running club, venture up to the 10 mile or half marathon distance. It had been over 25 years since I last ran a marathon. Several of my friends in the club had ventured beyond the marathon and I started to hear crazy stories about 50 mile and 100 mile races, and even an incredible race called the Badwater 135 that started in Death Valley and finished on Mt. Whitney. Then I start reading similar stories from my Runners World forum friends. The most fascinating thing about these stories was the way in which they portrayed an experience that to me, would be excruciatingly painful, as an incredible experience. Even, dare I say … fun. It also reminded me of the close-knit community that characterized distance runners before the first running boom in 1972. I was intrigued.

I decided to satisfy my curiosity and flew to Cleveland for the 2012 North Coast 24 Hour Run where about a dozen of my forum friends were running either the 12 hour or 24 hour race, and as many more were there for support crew and cheering. Under extremely adverse conditions including gale force winds strong enough to blow away tents, torrential rains, cold, and hail, my friends and the other runners persevered. More incredibly, some of them still kept smiles on their faces. The camaraderie was incredible and I began to understand that these ultra events were about more than just racing. Going into that race, my friends suggested I register that year, but on a base of 20 miles per week, I had no interest and wasn't tempted. After seeing what they accomplished on not a whole lot more than that, I realized that another year of training might make it feasible, so the idea started simmering in the back of my mind. I confided in one of the runners that I was considering it and got some encouraging feedback. Then December rolled around and registration opened. I think a dozen of my friends signed up the first day and the race has a cap of 200 for the combined 12 hour and 24 hour races. It still sounded crazy, but as the initial registration with a discounted entry fee was about to end, I committed myself. Now the question was what to do to prepare because I was just starting my indoor track season with my focus on the 800m and mile. That requires an entirely different mindset and training regime.

That is how I found myself, a middle distance runner, committed to running my first ultra marathon after almost 50 years of running. I was reluctant to move off the track onto the roads for longer races. I went into my first marathon back in 1970 dragging my heels while succumbing to peer pressure. At least marathons had been (somewhat) familiar territory, but an ultra marathon was completely beyond my ken. I hadn't the first inkling of where to start, except that I would need to run a lot more than I had been running during the indoor track season while racing 800m and the mile. My friends who ran ultras had gotten me into this, so ultimately I turned to them for advice. In a few cases the advice didn't make sense, so I continued to seek more information.

Along the way I assembled a list of almost a dozen websites, several books, and a few recommendations. I also began lurking on the ultra running forums. In the end, the most helpful suggestion was to hire a coach. I knew just the one, if he was willing to work with me. I had watched the progress of one of my friends and listened to her rave about her coach, so I decided that would be who I contacted first.

In my initial contact, I explained my somewhat unusual situation and training leading up to where I would be when starting training for my ultra. Somewhat to my surprise, he was willing to work with me anyway, and sent a long questionnaire about my background, training, health, expectations, and other relevant matters. Then we agreed to wait until the end of my indoor track season at the end of February followed by a short break in training for a vacation. That would give me six months to train.

I finally finished my indoor track season. While it wasn't everything I'd hoped for, overall I was satisfied, and I finished on a high note. After three months of intense speed training I looked forward to my vacation and a break from training before I commenced training for my 12 hour ultra. What I hadn't anticipated was getting sick on vacation and still being in recovery mode when I was supposed to be increasing my mileage and long runs.

When I engaged a coach and envisioned what the training would be like, I expected a gradual increase in weekly mileage with an emphasis on long runs. My conception of that was taking four to five of those months to increase my mileage from my current 30 miles per week to 50-60 miles per week and gradually bumping up my long run from seven miles to as many as 25 miles. I had also hoped to continue running intervals with my running club once a week and fit in some races along the way. The reality, however, was quite different.

My first two runs were supposed to be 5 and 8 miles. All I could manage was 2.1 and 5.7 miles. At the end of the week I was supposed to run 10 miles, a distance I hadn't run in a year and a half. I surprised myself and finished the workout with 10.1 miles. Over the next three weeks I handled the workouts well, including fartlek, tempo, and interval workouts. In three weeks my long run had almost doubled to 13 miles. I barely made it to 11 miles before I had to bail out. This was my first real setback and I began to wonder how I was going to manage even longer runs later in the schedule. When I looked at my schedule I had another 15 mile run 5 days later and my first 18 mile run 4 days after that followed by 19, 21, and 22 miles.

At that point I really had to trust that my coach knew what he was doing, because if left to myself I would have waited two weeks before attempting the 15 mile distance again. Since getting the miles in was the primary goal, we scheduled only two recovery runs over those four days. Going into the long run better rested made all the difference in the world. Four days later with two rest days and one recovery run, I tackled my first 18 mile run. This was a distance I had only run in training twice ever, both times over 40 years ago.

My first major checkpoint in my training, the Bob Potts Heritage Trail Marathon, was now only 5 weeks away. After the long runs I had a two week taper leading in to what would be my first marathon in over 30 years. If my coach hadn't come with such great credentials and high recommendations, I might have panicked. As it was I still had to play catch-up as I recovered from my illness and begin my adaptations to both the physical training and the change in mindset. Walking was no longer to be considered a last resort when I couldn't run anymore: now it was supposed to be an integral part of training and a key strategy to success. As training progressed, I was to find this shift in mindset my biggest challenge.

I now understood why so many novices wonder how they'll be able to complete their marathon when the long runs are so difficult to complete and they leave one 6-8 miles short of the marathon distance. Even with the marathon that close there was no letup in the training schedule yet. Basically, the marathon was supposed to be a supported training run rather than a goal race.

Of my three long training runs of 19, 21, and 22 miles, I only had to cut short the 22 mile run by two miles. When I stopped to refuel and drink at 20 miles, I couldn't muster the energy to get moving again for the final two miles. Training finally eased up a little with only an 11 mile run the week before the marathon.

Marathon day could not have been more perfect: cool, slightly overcast, a flat, fast course, great race organization, and incredible volunteers at the aid stations who were just as enthusiastic when I ran by as when the leaders had passed hours before. After finishing the Bob Potts Marathon my confidence was high. I recovered quickly from that effort and over the following three weeks I was hitting my paces and distances consistently. Training included some tough tempo, progression, and fartlek runs. With my middle distance background I found those to be easier than the long runs. Then I blew up and crashed 15 miles into a 17 mile run. It was all I could do to keep moving and finish the run.

Anyone can have bad run now and then and I'd been running some pretty tough workouts, so it wasn't surprising that I might have accumulated some fatigue. My next long run was a 20-miler where I was supposed to run every fourth mile faster. This was the hardest workout yet, combining both distance and some hard running. I was hitting my paces well but it was taking a toll on me. By mile 16 when I finished my fourth hard mile it was feeling more like a race effort than a training effort. On my final mile I continued to push the pace and was still on target with only a half mile to go when I hit a wall. I dropped from 10:45 pace to 13 or 14 minute pace in the space of a few strides and shuffled back to the finish. I took it easy the next few days and then had another short but hard workout. While I hit my paces again, it was a much harder effort than a training run should be.

The training was beginning to take a real toll on me. Even with the next two days off, I wasn't feeling rested. That weekend I was supposed to run my first set of back-to-back 18 mile long runs. On the first I started to fade at 7 miles and was able to make it only as far as 10 miles before I had to stop. The next day I covered the entire 18 miles, but only because I ran an out-and-back course and had no choice. The first 13 miles weren't too bad, but by the time I reached 15 miles I was walking more than running and the last 3 miles were almost all walking. After the highs of the marathon and the tough quality workouts I had run, I was at a low point. It was also only five days until my next checkpoint race, a 15K on July 4th where I had originally hope to run 1:33. At this point that looked entirely out of the question and I was wondering if I could even run 1:43.

After consulting with my coach we decided I needed an extended period to recover. Aside from a short shakedown run to work out some of the soreness from the back-to-back runs, I rested until race day. As expected, the weather was warm and humid. I did some quick assessments and decided to start at half marathon pace and see how the race developed. I readjusted my goal to break 1:40 and finished comfortably under that. That did a lot to restore my confidence but I had a lot to work on with the long runs and dealing with the heat.

I had just over three weeks until my next race, the Endless Summer 6-Hour Run in Annapolis, Maryland. We kept my workouts fairly short with no more long runs until then. We were in the middle of a heat wave. By the time temperatures finally broke, which wasn't until early August, we had 30 straight days where it never got below 70 degrees Fahrenheit, even overnight. I spent much of that period trying to learn better how to deal with the heat. I had to stop early on several workouts because of it and was hoping that we might have a break before race day. I fretted that I couldn't get in any long runs, but I wanted to be rested for the race. I had hopes of completing 7 loops of the 4.15 mile course for a total of 29.05 miles.

Initial weather reports were predicting slightly little cooler temperatures with the start in the high 60s and the finish only in the low 80s. I was caught off guard with the course being hillier than expected, as well as temperatures climbing faster and higher than anticipated. To my detriment, I was so set in what I wanted to accomplish that I refused to make the adjustments I should have made. By the end of my fourth lap I was in no condition to continue. Even if I hadn't realized that, the volunteers did and escorted me to the side where they ministered to me until I felt better. At that point I don't think I could have done more than walk another lap and saw no point in doing that. My final result was officially 16.6 miles and last place. Now I was really questioning whether I would or could be ready for North Coast 24. It was only 8 weeks away and my training and racing was getting worse, not better.

Over my first two months of training I had made strides I could never have envisioned. It hadn't been easy--especially the rapidly increasing length of the long runs--but it had culminated in what was, for me, a fantastic race at the Bob Potts Heritage Trail Marathon. Then the next two months had put me in a downward spiral reaching a nadir at the Endless Summer 6-Hour Run. It was time to regroup, consult with my coach, and make adjustments to my training. It didn't help that I was having issues with the heat and this was one of the hottest summers I'd experienced in recent years.

After discussing the issues with my coach, we noted that while I could run the quality workouts well, it took me longer to recover from them than from the long runs, even though I struggled more with the long runs. The more critical issue at the moment, though, was the heat. I purchased some wraps that could be frozen, then placed on my neck as needed, as well as ice packs. Then we spent a week allowing me to fully recover from the Endless Summer race before scheduling another long run. During that time we also experimented with finding a better run/walk ratio. While I agreed verbally that walk breaks were important, I still hadn't fully modified my long time disdain of them and kept trying to minimize and rush through them. Now being better equipped to deal with the heat I also adjusted my run/walk ratio to one to one for that week.

While my average pace with walk breaks was a lot slower than my normal pace for short runs, it wasn't that much slower than that of some of my long runs. It still remained to be seen how it would work when I actually resumed my long runs. The first test came 8 days after the race. Sure enough at about 14 miles I was hit with both the heat and fatigue despite slightly more frequent walk breaks. I took an extended break to ice my neck and drink cold fluids, then was able to continue 4 miles more to complete the run. The next 4 days were spent recovering before I tackled a hard ladder series on the track. As usual I ran that workout well, hitting all my paces from the 1600m all the way down to the 200m.

Two days later I tried another set of back to back long runs.

I was not recovered and was hesitant to push too hard. After slowing to a slow jog for several miles I stopped after only 15 of the planned 20 miles. The next day was even worse. I covered only 12 of the planned 20 miles. With a week and a half to my next marathon, my final tune-up before race day, we cut my workouts back again and added a lot more power walking. Another Runners World friend had referred me to an article on walking in the July issue of Ultrarunning that proved very useful for this. Then, a couple days before the marathon, I came down with some sort of 24 hour bug. I would have considered skipping the race if it weren't for the circumstances -- I desperately needed something to boost my confidence. The marathon was scheduled for a Friday morning, so I had to drive up to Nyack, New York on Thursday. If that day was an omen, it wasn't a good one. Even before leaving Pennsylvania I drove through rain that was coming down so hard I would have pulled over to wait it out if I could have seen well enough to change lanes.

Once I arrived in Nyack and had checked in, I drove out to the park where the race would be run. I had received good second hand reports that the race was very flat. I began to question that after driving over several daunting hills on the way to the park. There wasn't any way to drive the course, so I had to trust the reports. When I returned to the motel the power was out: no lights, no TV. At least dinner went well. I found a small Italian restaurant in town. Power was on when I got back, so I read a while then went to bed after setting the alarm. Friday morning I awoke to ... silence. No alarm. I frantically checked the time and was able to relax. I'd only overslept by 10-15 minutes. That didn't really matter because I was ready before breakfast was set out at 6:00 am.

Once breakfast was over I drove to the park, picked up my bib and t-shirt, and tried to relax before the start. I started out with a moderately ambitious run/walk ratio of 9 minutes running to 3 minutes walking. As the race developed I had to run less and walk more. Eventually I realized that if I were to finish, I would need to walk an extended time, perhaps a couple of the 3 miles laps. Since my goal was to finish regardless of what it took, even if that was more than 6 hours, that's what I would do. With one lap to go I still had time to possibly finish under 6 hours, especially if I were able

114

to jog or run some of the last lap. I finished much stronger than I expected and ran more of the last lap than I thought I'd be able to run so I finished comfortably under 6 hours. Being able to not only finish, but finish in that fashion was just the boost I needed.

A few days after the race I got sick again so I cut back the mileage on some of the scheduled runs. Training was beginning to wind down now and soon I'd begin my taper. There was one last 20 mile run to complete. I was supposed to run it as if it were the first 20 miles of the race. This one I knocked off successfully. While it wasn't easy, it was by far the easiest of the long runs and didn't leave me exhausted. The final 13 days would be spent resting with a few easy runs and power walks to keep active. At this point I felt the same way many first time marathoners describe how they feel: anxious, excited, disbelieving, and anticipating. Next stop: 12 hour race!

How does one describe an experience like this? It's more than just a race; it's a final exam for graduation, a testimonial, a vacation, a holiday, a celebration all rolled into one. Let me take a deep breath and start with my preparations for the trip.

Last year I brought homemade fudge to the race and was told that was expected again this year. I also innocently mentioned that I might make homemade Chex Mix as well. Wednesday evening found me mixing together ingredients. I only had time to make the Chex Mix on Wednesday, so Thursday morning saw me hovering over the stove with my fudge, making sure I didn't cook it for too long. I make the old-fashioned fudge with Hershey's cocoa… the good kind!

I still had to finish packing then triple check to make sure I hadn't left anything critical behind. I was aware that, most likely I was over packed and wouldn't use but a third of what I brought. Still… better to be safe than sorry. Really, as long as I had my shoes, anything else I could get in Cleveland if I had to.

I was hoping to be on the road shortly after noon on Thursday instead of waiting for Friday. I'd been fine at my other races after driving 2-3 hours the day before, but this would be an all day trip and I expected to be stiff and maybe even a little sluggish the next day. Even if I only got part way there, as long as I could cut Friday's driving to a couple hours, that would improve my chances of a better race. It was an added and unplanned expense, but with everything from the money to the sweat and tears that I had already put into this so far, it was worth it to me.

Yes! I was on the road at 1:30pm. I knew I should at least get to Ohio before I stopped for the night. As I expected, it took me longer than Yahoo! Maps said it would. I was more than ready to pull off the turnpike and find a room for the night. At least I could sleep in Friday morning and take my time driving the remainder of the distance, then relax for the rest of the day. As it happened I arrived in Cleveland hours before I could check into the hotel, so I drove to Edgewater Park where the race was being held and walked the loop several times. That served several purposes. It helped me unwind from the drive, reminded me of the layout and where I could expect wind coming off the lake, and where those little bumps in the course were that I was told would morph into mountains later in the race.

Afterwards I grabbed some lunch at a little Mexican restaurant before heading back to the park to relax. I spent a relaxing afternoon watching some locals play lightning chess. It was just what I needed to get my mind off the race for a while. Now I could finally check into my room and relax until our evening "FE" (forum encounter) and pre-race pizza party. At least a dozen of us were there I think, some of whom I was meeting in person for the first time and some whom I had met last year.

We had a great time sharing stories, pizza, and other goodies before heading back to our various hotels for what would hopefully be a good night's sleep or at least rest. I barely slept Friday night. It seemed like every time I woke, only a half hour or hour had passed. I finally gave in and got up at 6:00 a.m., dressed for the weather -- it was raining of course -- and went down to grab some breakfast. It wasn't a great selection but a couple muffins, an orange, and coffee would suffice for now. I knew there would be plenty of food at the race.

Several of my friends and a couple other runners I didn't know came in while I was there. I may have been one of the last to actually leave for the race, but there was still plenty of time. I had planned to get there about an hour before the start to pick up my packet and meet everyone. That should have been a simple task since this race is so well organized. After filling out a waiver I stood at the registration table waiting for someone to bring me my packet. I was puzzled when one of the volunteers asked if I'd gotten my packet yet. When I replied no, she went to look again for it and it was nowhere to be found. Apparently in a rush another runner had grabbed it and already left the area. Once we figured out who it was they paged him, but to no avail. I waited patiently while the RD and volunteer made sure they had a chip for me, gave me a new number, changed all the information on the other runner, and assured me all would be fine and that my laps and results would be recorded properly. Relieved and assured I finally walked down to our canopy and tents to greet everyone.

We had the obligatory pre-race photos of the group, including one with almost all of us sporting large fuzzy orange mustaches stuck to our upper lips. Race time neared so I made a last minute stop at the restroom before lining up near the back of the field. I think we had 152 runners registered for the two races and 117 who were able to make it to the starting line - 17 in the 12-hour race and 115 in the 24-hour race. This is where it starts to get hard, both the running and the writing. Based on my last long run which was supposed to be a dress rehearsal for the first 20 miles today, I began with alternating 5 minutes running and 3 minutes walking.

The first things I noticed was that I was running much faster than I expected and initially this had me worried. I decided I had to go with what felt right, not what my Garmin said, and this felt very easy and comfortable. Then I realized my planned pattern would conflict on some laps with stopping at the aid table. I also wanted to walk the two tiny inclines as much as possible because I'd been forewarned that they could seem like small mountains by the end of the race. This required a second decision on how to fit my run/walk pattern to the course. What seemed to work best was to extend the run by no more than 30 seconds or cut it back by 30-60 seconds so that I could walk through the aid station and hopefully finish that segment at the top of the first little hill. As long as I was running approximately 60% of each lap and walking the other 40%, I figured I would be okay. That's the way it stood for the first 40 laps, by which time it had finally stopped raining. The wind, however, did not ease and every time we approached the little downhill just before the finish we were smacked in the face with what felt like a gale force wind coming off Lake Erie. Since that coincided with one of my walk breaks, most of the time it was less of a factor than it could have been.

Meanwhile I was seeing our runners on the course and our support team every lap. I was trying to take in fluids and calories beginning at the end of lap two. My support team kept urging me to eat and drink more and asking if I needed anything. I tried but when I ate and drank more I started to feel bloated so I cut back again. I think this became a major factor later in the race. At one point one of the leaders passed me while I was walking and looked back over his shoulder to tell me my arm swing was unbalanced and that I should swing my right arm more. That was probably a habit I developed on my solo training runs when I often had to carry a bottle with me. I followed the advice and immediately noticed a difference in the ease of my walking. This was only one example of the help and encouragement I received along the way from friends and strangers, if you can call someone sharing this experience a stranger.

Another one of the top runners, one of the women leaders, had an encouraging comment every time she passed me. She was one of the runners I was later able to track down and thank personally for her help. I started to notice that the fatigue that had been building was finally affecting my pace significantly somewhere around the 40th lap or 36th mile. At this time I was probably about 2 to 3 miles ahead of schedule for a 50 mile total. I suspect that how I was feeling was reflected in my appearance. I dropped to almost even splits between running and walking, then shifted the emphasis to walking more than running. At this point the temptation to quit was very strong. I qualified as an ultra runner. I had not only passed 50K, I was well beyond that. I was nearing 40 miles. Did it really mean that much to reach 50 miles?

It was somewhere around that time that one of my guardian angels rejoined me and continued to walk with me stride for stride, lap after lap. I was discouraged and hurting, but her inspiration and caring concern reminded me that all I needed to do was keep putting one foot in front of the other. Just finish this lap first, then the next lap would take care of itself. She asked what I wanted as we reached the aid station and grabbed it for me so I would not lose my momentum.

Somewhere in those laps, I think around lap 42 or 43, one of my support crew squealed to the medical tent staff who sent someone out to politely but firmly suggest I come into the med tent to let them check on me. I turned to my guardian angel and inspiration for her advice, then it sunk in that I wasn't the best judge of my condition and meekly allowed myself to be escorted into the tent. They stretched me, questioned me, and had Dr. Lovey take a good look at me. When they finally let me go after 12-14 minutes, I had strict orders on what to eat and drink, not simply eat and drink more. When I resumed walking - I wasn't about to try running again and risk undoing all the good they had worked on me - my two guardian angels flanked me and made sure I got everything I needed. They continued to pace me through the finals laps and miles checking frequently on me to be sure I was still okay.

Each lap I could see that I was losing ground. Between that and the time spent in the med tent, I saw my hopes of 50 miles gradually fading. It was more important to me to be on my feet and still moving at the end than to pursue the 50 miles and risk a collapse so I moderated my pace to a level that I was reasonably confident I could hold. Amazingly to me, my guardian angels continued to comment on how well I was moving when I felt I was almost at a casual stroll. My final last full lap came at 55 laps and about 11:56:50. I desperately wanted to complete 50 miles so we continued one more unofficial lap. My guardian angel made a point of timing the next .4 miles so I would have at least an unofficial time of 12:01:53 for 50 miles.

I finished my unofficial 56th lap at 12:11:04 for 50.5 miles total. After a trip to the restroom, I thought it best to check back in with the medical staff. They sat me down on one of the tables to check me over. Within minutes I started to feel light-headed and a little dizzy. I felt washed out and was shivering, and had to lay down. My little visit to check in with them turned into a two hour stay while they ministered to me until they were satisfied that I was okay. I was supplied with Gatorade, bananas, hot vegetable broth, and protein in the form of a hamburger. I tried a hot dog too but couldn't stomach that. One of my guardian angels had to leave but the other stayed with me the entire time after going out to get me something dry and warm to change into. The medical staff kept chatting with me to keep up my spirits. I think it may also have been a clue to my condition because they seemed less worried.

When I responded more and also started joking a bit with them, they finally were satisfied that I was okay and let me go. One of the other 24-hour runners in our group who was going back to her hotel for an extended nap drove me back to mine. I barely remember climbing into bed. The next thing I remember was my phone ringing. When I finally realized what that noise was and answered, it was her reminding me it was time to head back to the race to see the rest of the runners finish. I think I surprised her that I felt well enough to drive, but we did get back to see some amazing final laps. I think she went back for a few more herself. I was still euphoric about mine. I also tried to make it a point to thank everyone I could find who had helped me, runners, support crew, runners' family, volunteers, RD, med people. I especially wanted to let the med people know I was fine. They obviously care about every single runner who came to them.

As I write this, it is now three days later and I'm still overwhelmed by the event and results. I've spent much of that time on the running forums catching up with everyone's race reports and comments and the race commentary posted on our Facebook groups. I've also managed to jog over Monday (yes, I could jog that soon after) to share my results with the cross country team. I promised my coach a full report and emailed my running club coach to let him know the results. One of the best parts was calling my daughter and being able to share all this with her. While I won't see my doctor until my next regular checkup in December, she'll also want to know how it went. Despite not being a runner, she has taken a strong interest in it and supports my running, even crazy events like this.

That about wraps it up though I'm sure I've forgotten a lot and my apologies to anyone I've overlooked who contributed to my success. At this point I'm still basking in the satisfaction on what I accomplished. I have no definite ideas about where I'll go from here or whether I'll ever run another ultra. This one is the most memorable races I've ever run among the 888 that I have in my race log, more so than even my first sub-5:00 mile and first sub-3:00 marathon, which was also my first marathon and at Boston as well. I don't see any rush to decide because my options are wide open from returning to the middle distances to maybe trying a trail 50K or anything in between. It's been a pleasure recording this journey so I can go back and remind myself of what it took and what it meant to me. If those of you who read it have also enjoyed or benefitted from it, all the better. Thank you.

The Cost

karen fennie

I wish you knew the value of one kind word
Like you know the value of that antique in the corner
The painting on the wall
The bright stones that shine on my right, ring finger

But kindness, some gentleness, requires no price
It's worth difficult to discern
The payback is uncertain, yes
I understand that
The risk to open your heart, even the tiniest bit
To admit, while there is darkness and disappointment, light pours
in every day
A reminder there is something else too

Surely by now you must know the cost of each brick in that
insurmountable wall

Run4Water 2017: My Masterpiece
bob hearn

Sunday, April 9, 2017

In the world of the game Go, there is the concept of a player's "masterpiece" – a game where you play flawlessly, yet lose by a single point. This race was my masterpiece. For once, I executed it absolutely perfectly, in my opinion. I would not change a thing. But it was not quite enough.

Background

For the past two and a half years, my primary running goal has been to make the U.S. national 24-hour team and represent my country at the World Championships. I was originally inspired by my friend Mike Henze, who helped pull the 2010 team to bronze in Brive, France.

My first attempt in December 2014 yielded 139.5 miles, 5.5 short of making the 2015 team. But it did show that I had potential, at least. I looked forward to 2016. But then, the IAU switched the World Championships to every other year – I would have to wait two more years. At Desert Solstice in December 2015, I ran 149.24, putting me in the number four spot, of six, for 2017. But there was over a year left to qualify, and I thought that likely would not hold. The two-year wait meant more interest for fewer (average) slots. As well, the level of U.S. 24-hour talent seemed to be on the rise.

Since then it has been a constant game of learning what I can from the previous race, and applying the lessons to the next race. It's a slow way to learn, with a pretty big cost per data point. But as an older runner (now 51) without a surplus of natural talent, my only chance here is to run smarter and execute better than my competitors. Anything shorter, I am just too slow to be competitive at the national level. But 24-hour is about a lot more than talent and speed.

Gradually, I have been able to put together races that go perfectly for longer and longer into the race. At Riverbank, five weeks ago, I was perfect through 16 hours, hitting 100 miles at 15:30 (a big PR), exactly on my planned paces. And I still felt good; nothing hurt at all. But then I suddenly became very mentally fatigued. I walked a few laps to try to get a reset, giving up some of my possible upside. I hung on through 20 hours with some effort, but by then the difficulty in focusing was extreme – though still with no real physical pain, which seemed remarkable to me. That, at least, was a first. I thought a shot of more sugar might help jolt me awake, but instead it made me puke, which sapped all my remaining mental reserves. I mostly walked it in after that. Rich Riopel ran 152.21, finally bumping me from number four to number five. Well, I was amazed my spot had held for over a year.

Riverbank had been, I thought, my last chance. There were only five weeks left to qualify, too close to try again after an all-out effort. But my performance there had left a bad taste in my mouth. Not because I didn't hit my goal, but because I couldn't convince myself that I hadn't given up too easily. The going got tough, and I didn't handle it. Those are the moments when we are supposed to truly live as runners, and test our souls. It had been crystal clear to me that here it was, right in front of me, everything I had worked hard for years, on the line. All I had to do was hold it NOW, for just a few more hours. I would be the first American over 50 to break 150 miles. I would virtually secure my team spot. And yet, I really, really wanted an excuse to quit. And I got the excuse, when I puked.

After that experience, my identity and validity as a runner were in question. That's what really hurt. And yet – where is the line between physical failure and mental failure? The brain is not immune from the laws of physics. My feeling was that this was largely nutritional. I'm not supposed to be that tired and unfocused at any point in a 24-hour. I'm very good at the objective, analytical part of running, at least for certain types of events. And I generally feel like I'm good at the subjective part too; I'm tough when I need to be. But your brain can only do what it can do, too.

Over the next couple of weeks, my recovery went quicker

than expected; everything felt great. I had obvious nutritional and other tweaks to make after Riverbank – again, I wanted a do-over. (Riverbank had been my do-over from Desert Solstice in December.) And Greg Armstrong let me know there was still a space for me at Run4Water. The line-up of real challengers there was growing, and I couldn't help but feel my #5 spot was at serious risk. I went so far as to write a little program to estimate the chances that at least two guys ran over 149.24: it said 64%. Hmm. Well, what did I have to lose? So I made the decision to give it one final shot.

The Race

Run4Water is run on a .508-mile road loop in Lebanon, TN, around a middle school. It's not 100% flat, but pretty close. The slight variation might serve to change it up a bit for our muscles. The weather in Tennessee on April 1st could be anything, but would likely be warm and humid, maybe with rain. That's what I should have hoped for to secure my spot! It generally takes good conditions to see good performances. Nobody in the U.S. broke 150 for all of 2016, primarily I think because no race had really good conditions.

But I was torn. I had really wanted a solid performance over 150 to give me confidence to shoot higher at Worlds. I was getting pretty tired of coming up short. Fortunately, or unfortunately, the closer race day got, the better the forecast looked. With the likes of Jon Olsen, Steve Slaby, Phil McCarthy, Greg Soutiea, Josh Finger, Olaf Wasternack, Joe Fejes, Adrian Stanciu, and a few other fast guys toeing the line, it looked like a day for potentially big numbers. One day later, and it would have been high 70s and thunderstorms.

So, I had made the right decision. I had to step up here to keep my spot. If I finished in the top two I was guaranteed at least the 6th slot. If two people beat me, then I would have to pass Rich's 152.21. I dialed in my pacing plan so that if all went smoothly, I'd hit 153.43. If I felt great towards the end I could go for more, but that was not the priority. If three people beat me... well, let's not go there.

8 am, and we were off. With this concentration of talent, I'd

been hoping to see a fast start, with nobody wanting to get too far behind. That would work very well for me, as I waited patiently for the inevitable attrition. Almost everyone goes out too fast at 24-hour. But if I'd hoped all my competition would blow up early, I was out of luck. A few shot off way too fast, but others reined it in instead. Olsen was completely out of my equations – his talent and experience were far above everyone else's. (Incidentally Olsen was also the race director at Riverbank.) If he had no injury issues or bad luck, he would easily make the team; he was in charge of his own fate. Everyone else had to have a very good day, and were racing each other for that 6th spot.

Still, after a couple of hours the order settled down, and I found myself 11th man, with all of my expected competition ahead of me. Perfect, exactly where I wanted to be. Most people in this position would feel scared, especially as the early pacing feels soooooo easy. But I knew that I was not going too slow. If I held this pace I'd hit a big PR, and a number almost certainly good enough to make the team. Any faster would be unnecessary risk. Ergo, most of my competition were taking unnecessary risks; advantage Bob.

In the week or so before the race, after I'd decided I felt good and committed to it, a few of my chronic muscle issues had begun to rear their heads again, so I was just a bit concerned about that. Indeed, in the first several hours lots of things felt not quite right. The worst was the left hamstring, where I tore the tendons a few years ago. But I know that this tends to settle down after 30 miles or so in races, so I just sat back on my pacing and didn't sweat it.

This is the kind of thing that can mess with your head if you let it. 24 hours is a long time to stay focused, especially when your margin for success is so razor thin. It's all too easy to convince yourself that it's just not going to be your day, and that feeling can become a self-fulfilling prophecy. This is true in any long ultra, but it's magnified at 24-hour, because you know that there's not going to be any change of terrain to mix things up, and you have to fight the sheer boredom and repetitiveness of a short loop. Unlike a fixed-distance race, the finish does not get any closer no matter how fast you run, and there's no such thing as a black-and-white finish vs. DNF to motivate you – your result is simply however far you ran. It adds up to a unique set of mental challenges.

And really, mental toughness was my biggest concern coming into Run4Water. I had gone all out in very long races way too much recently: this was my third 24-hour in four months, with Spartathlon just a couple of months prior, all of them A races. You can only go to the well so often. Especially as I thought I had not been tough enough at Riverbank, I was afraid I just wouldn't be able to step up here. But the edge I had this time was the sure knowledge that this was it; it would all be determined here this weekend.

The laps clicked off, and the day progressed. Early on we heard what sounded like a tornado alarm. Tornado?? Well that would save my team spot! No such luck, though. I should mention here the perfect logistics Greg had arranged. Portapotties were immediately alongside the course, and crew access was ideal, near the timing mat. Volunteers were available for anything you might need. My morning crew of Tanya and Cheryl made things easy for me. My pattern was to run 4:36 laps (9:03 mile pace), and walk one minute every third lap. During the walk breaks I would drink and fuel. I'd grab a small bottle from my crew, then toss it in a bin just before running again, whence my crew would retrieve and refill it. Maximally efficient. Also the tracking page had a way to send messages to the runners; my crew called them out to me again and again. I went back and looked, as the messages are logged with the results. It seems I had a lot more support messages than anyone else. I had no idea I was so popular! Thank you, Running Ahead crew, Facebook friends, and Liz!

Around 2 pm my afternoon crew of Kara and Tim showed up to relieve Tanya and Cheryl, as we switched direction from clockwise to counter-clockwise. The six-hour switches helped keep things fresh; it's like running a new course. Things were still going smoothly for me. The day was cool and overcast. We were supposed to get clear skies and mid-60s in the afternoon, but when we finally did, we still had a brisk breeze to offset the sun. A few people did seem to be affected by the heat, but I guess my sauna training plus the breeze meant that I barely noticed it. I came prepared with lots of ice and sponges, but didn't use them.

I enjoyed chatting with friends and getting to know new people throughout the day; the first hours of a 24-hour are comfortable and social for everyone. Before the race I had finally met Roy Pirrung, an ultrarunning legend, with many age-group records, and also one of the first Americans to have run Spartathlon.

After 8 or so hours the early leaders started to drop off, and I gradually began climbing through the ranks. My 12-hour split was about 77 miles, right on target. Before much longer it was down to Jon Olsen, Steve Slaby, and Greg Soutiea ahead of me. All of them still had several laps on me; I wouldn't be catching anyone else soon. I had promised myself I would run my own race until at least 16 hours before considering the tactical situation with the other runners, but it was hard not to look ahead. Yes, it was still early, but... if everyone stayed strong, 153 would not be enough. I would instead have to hit Harvey Lewis' mark of 157.91 to stay on the team if I finished in 4th. That would be a huge challenge, even pacing to hit it from here – a 77 / 81 split. It would be virtually impossible if I waited until 16 hours to speed up. I considered asking Tracey Outlaw to run the numbers for me; I'd left him with my magic pacing spreadsheet. But then I came to my senses. It was very unlikely for all three ahead of me to hit 158. In fact Greg had already slowed and was now maintaining his 8-lap lead on me, not gaining further. He was no longer on pace to pass Harvey. Whereas if I sped up substantially now, the risk would be high that I'd blow up. As far as I can tell, actually, there had never been a single race in U.S. history with three men over 150, let alone 158. (Desert Solstice 2014 had three total over 150, but that included Katalin Nagy.)

So, I just had to hang tight for now, and make sure I eventually caught somebody, probably Greg. Jon was in his own world, but I'd thought both Steve and Greg had gone out faster than necessary. Steve was only running his second 24-hour, and had loads of talent and speed that was yet to be optimally applied here, so it was hard to know what his potential was. But Greg had run several, with a big PR of 143+ at Desert Solstice in December. That race had seemed to go very smoothly for him, and he'd had to work hard for it; he had no obvious mistakes to correct, or untapped reserves to apply here, at least that I was aware of. To have a shot at the team he had no choice but to attempt another huge PR, but he was actually aiming much higher. He just had to beat Rich's 152.21, and beat me. The four miles he was ahead of me here would have to be paid for, I was increasingly sure.

At 10 pm Kara and Tim headed back to Alabama (thank you!), and Sue Scholl, veteran of many ultras, took over as crew. She hadn't planned to stay all night, but wound up helping me through the end of the race, and beyond. Thank you, Sue! As a very experienced ultrarunner and crewperson, she anticipated my every need.

As we approached 16 hours, still easy and smooth for me, I looked back to Riverbank, where it seemed a switch had flipped at that point. Here I took a preventative NoDoz, the first time I'd tried that in a race. Normally I get my caffeine from Coke, but that's not as much, or as big a hit at once. I think I have a natural advantage in this kind of race due to my programming background. I pulled tons of all-nighters in college, and even much more recently at startups. I'm good running through the night, and also good focusing on tasks that would mentally exhaust others. However, lately I've begun to struggle more with tiredness; the years are beginning to add up. So I took no chances.

So far, so good, still holding steady. Now I was in new terrain, farther into the race still completely on track than I'd ever been before. It had been dark now for several hours, and this hit me harder than I had expected. There were street lights, but long stretches of the loop were pretty dark. Not dark enough not to see where to run – you had to watch out for the occasional speed bumps, but that wasn't too hard. However, I was accustomed to more light, having run most of my 24s on a track. I had to fight a bit mentally not to be slowed by this. When you run through the night in a trail race, you naturally slow; no big deal, everyone does. But I didn't have the margin in my pacing plan here to slow any.

From here on out, I know, it gets increasingly difficult. More than once I thought back to the words of Mike Henze, my friend from the 2010 team:

"The two decent races I ran - They would have to pulled me off in a hearse to stop my focus and drive toward my goals. I did not care if I died - Nothing was going to get in my way."

I could hope that the pace would feel easy the rest of the way, and the only question would be how much extra to go for, but realistically I would probably have to dig deep at some point, and I wanted to be ready to step up when the time came. Besides, there's how your body feels, and how your mind feels. The mind looks for excuses, even when the body is fine. I had already gone through many emotional ups and downs during the race, but that is normal, and habit kept me moving forward steadily.

Very gradually, I began to catch up to Greg. It took maybe an hour per lap to catch up. At this rate I would just catch him by the end of the race, but I could tell he was already struggling to hold on, whereas I was still holding back, prepared to speed up if necessary. And by about 18 hours it was all over for him.

So – endgame. Everything was now clear. Jon and Steve looked good to stay ahead of me and qualify. Steve could still falter, but it was looking unlikely. Nobody else was within reach of Rich's mark, so all that was left in the qualification picture, on the men's side, was whether or not I could catch Rich. For the one race that mattered, the guy I had to catch wasn't even physically in the race. But his presence was certainly felt. On the women's side, it was already settled. Gina Slaby would easily clear 140, bumping Megan Alvarado from her 6th-place spot. Megan was also in the race, as was #8 Laurie Dymond, but they had struggled early and were now out of contention. Unprecedented, shocking, that 140 was not good enough to make the women's team, or 150 the men's team.

At 19:23, I broke my own age-group 200-km record by over 13 minutes – or so I thought. Later I remembered that USATF only recognizes a track, not road, record here.

20 hours – I take another NoDoz. 21 hours – now I am beginning to feel it. I do some mental math, and decide it's time to use a bit of my cushion for safety. I will finally break that magic 150, at least, but there will be no padding of my record this time. I walk a little longer on the walk breaks. All is still well... until 22 hours.

I have always believed that 24-hour performance is ultimately limited by cumulative muscle damage. You think you are in a steady state, running a "forever" pace, no lactate accumulation to worry about. But it doesn't work that way. Eventually all the microtrauma even from the forever pace adds up, and you have to slow down. By starting at as slow a pace as possible for my goals, with walk breaks as well, I had deferred this point as long as possible. But here it was. Gradually, my legs began to fail. I had to take increasingly frequent walk breaks. If I didn't, my legs would buckle. My model of what was going on here is that my pool of muscle fibers able to perform at the level of my demand had dipped below a critical threshold. (Addendum – Trent Rosenbloom points out that the level of muscle damage I describe here ought to be accompanied by extreme muscle pain and rhabdomyolysis, neither of which I had. So, maybe it's back to the drawing board for other explanations. Fatigue is such a complex phenomenon.)

The pace chart shows the rest of the story. The tail there probably tracks some theoretical physiological curve of progressive muscle failure. I was now relying on that inspiration from Mike Henze, to keep pushing myself to the physiological limit. Everything was on the line here: I succeed, and the past years of work will all have been justified, all the failures wiped away in an instant. I fail, and it's all for nothing. It doesn't get any more stark than that.

My masterpiece.

Everyone else now knows what's going on; everyone is following as it appears my race is on a knife edge, and cheering loudly for me. Greg, Tracey Outlaw, Mike Dobies, and Bill Schultz are calling out lap splits I need to hit.

With maybe 20 minutes left, as I hit the timing mat and slow for a walk break, I collapse and grab the timing structure, just about taking it down with me. Back on my feet, keep pushing. Now, finally, I am beginning to lose faith that I will make it. I need at least 300 laps, and I'm going to be short. Greg tries to tell me no, you don't have to complete the 300th lap; a partial lap will do. But I don't believe him. I'd put all the relevant marks in a spreadsheet; I was sure 152.21 miles was 299.9 something laps. It was actually 299.34. So for the last two laps I think I am just fighting on principle, with no real chance, but Greg knows I still have a shot.

As I cross the mat for the last time, 299 done, I have about a minute and a half left. It's not enough. Even knowing two laps earlier where the actual mark was would have made no difference. I am confident I gave it everything I had – and I think anyone watching would agree.

The alarm sounds, and I collapse onto the grass. Greg goes back to wheel the partial lap, but there is really no need.

I finish with 152.155 miles, 300 feet short.

Aftermath

Greg, Sue, and others hover over me to make sure I'm OK. I just want to sleep. But people are worried about me, so after 10 or so minutes I let myself be helped up and back to the school. I am surprised to see a large crowd applauding as I enter, and am given a cot to recover on. I'm surprisingly unemotional about what has just happened; it's all too much to process. But there are a lot of not-dry eyes around me. It's humbling to have affected so many people.

How do I feel now about the years of effort, and coming up short in the end by the tiniest of margins? Above I said "I succeed, and the past years of work will all have been justified, all the failures wiped away in an instant. I fail, and it's all for nothing."

But in the end, it wasn't for nothing; I somehow found a third way. The unique circumstances here formed a crucible in which I was pushed to my absolute limits. And I didn't give up. If Rich's mark had been a hair higher, it would have been clearly out of reach sooner. A hair lower, and I'd have reached it, not really knowing if I had plumbed the absolute depths. But now I know. In a strange way, I feel fortunate to have been given this rare opportunity to create my "masterpiece".

Moreover, running is usually a selfish activity for me, but in this case it seems clear that I had a big effect on many other people, not just at the race but watching online, providing a source of motivation for their own races going forward. And that is immensely gratifying. I've been overwhelmed with the outpouring of thanks for my performance.

Finally, though it wasn't my primary goal, I did become the first American over 50 to break 150 miles. That is something I worked hard for and can be proud of.

Thank You

Thank you to my wonderful crew of Tanya Savory, Cheryl Renee Crowe, Kara Dudek Teacoach, Timothy Walters, and Sue Scholl (with further assistance from Tracey Outlaw and Bill Schultz) for your invaluable support. I'm indebted to all of you; you helped me execute this perfect race.

Thank you to everyone who was there and cheered me on. Thank you to everyone who watched online and was inspired. Thank you to my family and friends, especially Liz and Scott, who have supported me in this endeavor over the long haul.

Thank you to Greg Armstrong, for organizing an absolutely top-notch event in which to provide serious competitors one final shot to make the national team. Everything about the race was outstanding. Greg is a veteran of the 2015 team himself, and thoroughly understands all the concerns relevant to 24-hour runners. Race logistics issues were completely off the table for runners to have to worry about; everything just worked. And someone was always there for anything you needed. Moreover, I'm very appreciative of the personal interest Greg displayed in trying to give me every opportunity to solidify my spot.

What's Next?

I'm going to Worlds in Ireland. What? Yes, I was short, and didn't make the team. I'm first alternate. Possibly a spot will open up, probably not. But alternates are allowed to run in the race as well, just not as team members. And for the first time this year, the World Master's Association is hosting competition for world age-group titles. I can now compete on a more level playing field, with the best 50-54 runners.

Realistically, I would have been at best a strong backup member on the team anyway. Six are on the team, but only the top three scores count. With the amazing, unprecedented strength of this year's team (men and women), that was unlikely to be me. The age-group title is something I can get behind. I will have some serious competition there, but I am definitely going to be in the mix. And I'm incredibly excited about that.

I'll close with these words from Mike Henze, who independently arrived at the "masterpiece" metaphor.

Speed and Endurance and the amount you have of each is the baseline for performance or the canvas.

The race strategy and sticking to it gives you brushes and technique. The problem solving on the fly are the choice of colors.

The true beauty is in how you put everything together and the human spirit and effort you give to the race.

Sometimes you paint a crappy picture and sometimes a good picture - But each time you race it is a beautiful experience of self-discovery.

Then if the stars align and you find that absolute conviction ... You paint a masterpiece.

This Road I Run On
dallas smith

The question I get most often for someone I haven't seen in a while is: "Are you still running?" I don't mind that question. I understand where it comes from. "Are you still running?" Yes. Still living, too. For me maybe the two are the same.

The next question I get: "Don't you ever have trouble with your knees?" Well, no. My knees have been running a great long time. They adapted, growing muscle and sinew and cartilage and bone where it was needed for running. If I were a roofer spending the day climbing ladders and kneeling and hunkering, I'd have knee trouble. My knees are not trained for installing roofs. Roofing is not my job. Running is. My knees know my trade. Inactivity will not improve my knees.

I'm old. There's nothing new in being old. I've been old a long old time. My pace now is good only for a 78-year-old man, not for a 34-year-old man, as it was fourteen years ago, when I outran most thirty-something runners, pushing six minutes a mile in a 5K. But, as I say, that was fourteen years ago.

Those days are gone. Now I find myself writing about being old. It's hard to know why I'd write about that. I can find only one reason. I am writing your future. It's your future written in my present and you can read it in your present. But I'm not sure how deeply you want to look into that pool. It grows murky.

Strictly speaking, my present is your future only in the first approximation. An engineer would say it that way, and I used to be one. Your story is not my story. You will have to live your own story. You will have to live your own truth and then find what you can say about it. Examine your future in my present with caution.

My truth is this road I run on. It has taken me places I never expected to go, to despair on a simmering, dusty trail in Spain, to an exultant sunset after a record-setting run in Hawaii. And a thousand places in between.

Today it takes me across town; across the Tennessee Tech campus, where walks wait quietly for the students to return from holidays; through the historic district down Dixie Avenue and its stately old houses; through Dogwood Park, past the winter-dormant fountain sitting quietly; through Cookeville City Cemetery, where an officer in his car comes nosing down as I drift among the tombstones, protecting the property, as he should - pockets in my running shorts are much too small to carry a stolen tombstone, and I have no need of such an object; through Darwin Houses, a government project where once I did reside in dispiriting poverty with a wife and a baby and a full course load and a great lack of money.

The road I run on took me to those places today and put 12 miles in time's infinite bag. Time's bag is infinite. Mine is finite.

But it's not full yet.

Departures

karen fennie

My friend calls this the season of loss
The age we have reached now
Of regular departures

I imagine loved ones
Perched on a cliff
Faces to the wind
Ready to take flight when their particular current arrives

I am standing at a distance
Waving my arms
Look here
Not yet
Stay please

Too many goodbyes
The sun blocked by all those wings
Come back

Palo Duro Canyon 50
dr. Lisa Butler

It was 3 a.m. Friday morning when I crated my beasties and loaded the car for the trek Southwest to Amarillo. The beasties are punishing me for leaving them at home with aromatic emissions as I type this ... no doubt due to a well-meaning neighbor who throws treats over the fence. I already digress ... but I have time to kill since this is my one watering day of the week and I have herbs that need a drink if they are to season our Thanksgiving feast in a month.

I arrived at Palo Duro Canyon at 11 a.m. to help race directors Red Spicer and Bill and Winn Ross set up for the next morning's race. They had the EZ-ups in place, the water barrels at the ready, the chalk lines across the roads and in the tricky spots. Final bits of tape were being hung like early Christmas ornaments to mark the way and Texas flags were being posted at various sites. Once they had everything out that they thought wouldn't be stolen, we headed back to Amarillo for Packet Pickup.

Packet Pickup is one of my favorite places to give a little help. I get to see nearly everyone before the race, collect hugs, visit with old friends, and welcome new ones. It was a perfect evening with a cool breeze, a bright half-moon, and happy runners enjoying a yummy pasta feed. And like so many other runners, I headed back to the Canyon to camp among the Indian Princesses and Boy Scouts under a canopy of stars.

Race morning was gloriously cool. I wrapped a fleece blanket around my legs until the start to keep warm. We gathered there on the grass, under the banner, flanked on one side by Texas Flags and on the other side by flags from the states of the participants, save our favorite Redneck whose flag was absent. The mini-briefing was given. Bill Ross, co-race director, explained to everyone that the Palo Duro Canyon 50 for this year was being held in Memory of Phil Spicer, son of RD Red Spicer. Phil died earlier this year of colon cancer. His aid station, Two Moons, was being manned by his sister.

After a moment of silence, the race was started and everyone took off into the dark before the dawn. Palo Duro Canyon is full of spirits... it whispers... We ran down Paseo Del Rio through a grove of cottonwood trees and along a river...past Shaliko's Cairn (you'd have to read the hysterical marker explaining it). Barely 1.5 miles to the first aid station – seems short until later loops. The 50 milers split off left toward the cliffs. The 50K'ers go right toward the Lighthouse formation. The trail is smooth, dry dirt; the hills, rolling. The light was nearly full by the time we reached the GSL turnoff.

This is my favorite part of the trail. It is lightly rolling, smooth trail. It is fast. It crosses several dry riverbeds and is flanked with a few fall wildflowers, prickly pear, and soapbush. About halfway around the loop was the next aid station known as Little Fox, but affectionately called "Dos Locos Senoritas" for the volunteers who work their crazy magic. Then on past Red Star Ridge and its canyon overlook to the start/finish/aid area below the windmill.

By then the 20K'ers had been off for 5 minutes so I got to run to catch up to a number of friends. This time at Two Moons I took the same route the 50 milers had taken an hour before. Across the road to Rojo Grande and its cinnamon cliffs, then a turn onto Juniper Creekside and across another road to the Juniper Cliffside trail. Along the cliffs to the Sunflower trail and back into Two Moons at about 7 miles into the loop. Then back out along Lighthouse and GSL for the next 5.5 miles.

It was beginning to get hot at that point and everyone was slowing down except the speed demons at the front of the 50K and 50 Mile pack. Despite the heat, many runner ran fast times. By the time I dragged my sorry butt across the finish line it was 88+ degrees. By the time the 50M finishers started coming in it was 93. The sun was beaming cheerfulness down on us all and braising us in our own sweat. It highlighted the red and white of the Spanish Skirts, Palo Duro's rocky cliffs. It coaxed fragrance from the Juniper. And it tanned those who had finished and were laying around the start/finish area like beached whales after gorging themselves on Primo's hamburgers.

Just as the sun began to relent a little, the last of the 50 milers finished. Happy runners picked up their finisher's caps and headed toward the showers to wash off the red dust. The finish line and aid stations were disassembled quickly by the volunteers. The runners reassembled for a post-race fajita dinner and awards. Red, a colorful southern gentleman, gave out the awards, embroidered denim jackets for the men and embroidered fleece sweatshirts for the women. Then there were the door prizes, so many of them. Heart rate monitors, jugs of gel, headlamps, jackets, gift certificates, original artwork, and the traditional watercolor of Sorensen Point (which stands directly across from the finish) with an original poem by Red.

Our little group, mostly North Texas Trail Runners, plus myself and the Redneck, sat around the campfire late into the night, telling stories, sighing a little when we wiggled our toes, and contemplating making s'mores (but deciding that it is morally wrong to waste Scharffenberger or Jamesions chocolate on sta-puffed marshmallows). We slept beneath the stars one more time ... and dreamt of next year's PD50.

Watching the DC Eagle Cam
karen fennie

Today might be a good day for the first flight
Is that what you're thinking balanced on the lip of the nest?
A moderate breeze is stirring the leaves
The branches are waving ever so gently
What will it feel like, I wonder, when those enormous, beautiful
wings catch air
And you find yourself sailing, terrified and joyful
Away from the only home you've ever known

Found on Ute Trail

dr. lisa butler

An Indian summer day on Ute trail
Sweat trickles down my neck
  like the Shaman's pony tail.
Aspens scatter their riches on the path,
  gold coins beside the dangerous red of poison ivy
  and sharp green soapbush.

I am the only warrior running this trail
  to the drumbeat of gunfire across the canyon.
I weave like the moaning cedar wind
  between the white and brown bones
  of Ancient Ones spreading their shade above me.
Unseen except for the gaze of a white-headed
  Grandfather mountain
  with a crescent of Grandmother moon at his shoulder.

Today I am in love with my life.
Where last night I ground my teeth
  beneath the weight of the stones I carry,
    here I am restored, but for a pair of shoes,
  and scatter my stones, runes,
    among the sun warmed boulders
    to change my fortunes.

In the embrace of a mountain fall,
  I am lifted.
Surely it is real medicine
  to be suckled on warm water and trail dust
  and know the pull of mother Earth
    on an uphill struggle.
When my soul is so full of this day
  that my legs will not carry me up one more mountain
  for the weight,
  I will rest
        until tomorrow's run.
there is magic in the simplest of things

Big Wheel Turning / Life Passing On
fred murolo

All:

I've been on the list for a while. Every day I read the birthday notices. I see the names of people who used to regularly contribute, but have been silent for months or years. Christian (who still posts something now and then), Steve the Sleeve, Addygrl, Don, Gillian (I even noticed Alan's daughter's birthday). People's lives change: they move, they are busy with something besides ultrarunning, they share their lives on some other form of social media. The list is less vibrant for their absence, but that's the way life is.

Then there are the actual passings. Yesterday Mike mentioned Matt Watts. Many mourned the passing of Stu, John M., Dan B., many others, some more timely, some way too soon, none easy.

Which brings me to Damon Lease. Years ago, Damon was a regular contributor to the List. He was a renaissance man: math major, IT man, ultrarunner, backwoods hiker, skier and ski instructor, fly fisherman, wine and fine food enthusiast. As with all of us he was also so much more. Among numerous ultras, he ran the Vermont 100 a few times and then was a fixture there as a volunteer.

Damon battled for years with the insidious and destructive liposarcoma, a cancer that you can treat, but never really get rid of. As with everything, he went at it straight ahead and with eyes open. He endured numerous treatments, surgeries, hospitalizations. Damon died on August 28th of this year. I think he was 58. Far too young.

I posted a little tribute to him on the list several months ago because I knew he was having some rough going, and I wanted him to know I appreciated the role he had played in welcoming me into the ultrarunning family. I'm reposting it below.

*****

Life flies by and so many things I want to post to the list languish and become untimely. This one still makes sense to me:

I read my friend Steve Tursi's birthday tribute to Andy Cable last week, and I thought we all have one person who reached out and made us feel welcome in the ultra family. Each of us started at some point not knowing anything and showing up at a race trying to figure out how to run and complete these things.

Many people have helped and offered advice along the way. But my person, the one whom I remember meeting on the literal eve of my first 100-mile attempt, is Damon Lease.

I loved running, but I knew nothing about long distances. I had private fantasies as we all probably do. Maybe, notwithstanding never running a marathon under 3:16, I would have some super-human ultra endurance. Maybe I could just go and go as the miles accrued. I would be an anomaly. Hah. We're all built the same inside, but a boy can dream.

I really knew no people in the sport, except a few I had met at the two ultras I had run. But there I was full of excitement and dread checking into the Vermont 100 in Silver Hill Meadow on a Friday in the middle of July, 2006. And there was Damon checking people in. He was friendly and talky and we talked a little about the forecast of high heat, Endurolytes and S-Caps, fueling and nutrition over long races in general. He was not that young (mid-40s), which was good to me because I was attempting my first 100 at 49. He was not an ectomorph, which was good because I had already been told I had more of a football body than a runner body. (I weighed in that day at pre-race weight of 184.) He was quietly experienced and confident about one's ability to run 100 miles. He had run Vermont previously, as well as Wasatch and Hardrock. And without any special proclamations or fanfare, Damon made me feel at ease. Like I could and would do this despite my being a rookie and being clueless as to what it would take to run 100 miles.

He ran the race the next day, and he finished. I dropped coming through Camp 10 Bear the second time at 68 miles. I had no idea how much tougher I needed to be to run 100 at Vermont.

I was back the next year and Damon was there and once again friendly and helpful. He warned me off ibuprofen during the race, especially on hot days. He finished again, as did I that year. I had figured it out just a bit. With a little help from my friends.

I've seen and talked to him since then. We became Facebook friends. Damon became one of the perennial volunteers, running Camp 10 Bear for a few years.

Damon has not done as much ultrarunning the last few years. He has done a lot of fly fishing. He's had some health issues as have many of us. Growing older is not for the faint of heart. So, I haven't seen him recently, but he will always be that guy who welcomed me into a community that changed my life for the better.

Thanks, Damon. Be good, my friend.

*****

Best to all.

Fred in CT (feeling the passing of the years today)

Running for My Life
scotty louise eckert

I was an athletic kid. I had skills in gymnastics, ice skating, swimming and diving but what I really wanted to do was run; sometimes to run and never stop. The first time I ran away from home I was 4 years old. I packed my mustard sandwiches and left after telling my mother good-bye. I returned home only because nature called and there were no bathrooms on my route. Some things never change.

My mother died of cancer when she was 42. She never got to meet my husband or her 3 grandchildren. She was full of piss and vinegar and I think that is where I got mine. After my mother died, I just felt like running until my heart gave out.

My father committed suicide when he was 54. It took him a year to die. He had emptied the medicine cabinet and one of the bottles he consumed contained diuretics which damaged his internal organs. His stomach was pumped out but nothing could be done about the organ damage. Although I think it was the bravest act my father ever committed, I felt like I was suffocating. I wanted to run and keep on running but life just got in the way.

I married my partner, John, a jazz musician in 1972. Because of his line of work he traveled a lot. When we could, our three children, Michael, Matthew and Elizabeth, and I would travel with him. I also took care of my invalid mother-in-law for 22 years and I worked a full-time job. Although I longed to run, circumstances made it out of the question at this time in my life.

Finally, when my kids were grown and my mother-in-law passed away, I started running again. I met my mentor, Darren Worts, at a club where we both worked. At 56, I thought I had gotten too old to attempt a marathon, but because Darren believed in me, he convinced me I could fulfill my lifelong dream of running a marathon. I trained for the Steamtown Marathon using a training schedule Darren gave me. I ran that marathon that year, my first race ever, thanks to Darren's unwavering belief in me.

My firstborn son, Michael, was an adventurer and traveled for a while after he graduated from high school. He experienced life at its fullest before he decided it was time to further his education. He attended Stanford University and graduated with a degree in chemical engineering.

To celebrate his graduation he decided to go on a whitewater rafting trip on the Tuolumne River in CA. He had made this trip before; however, this year, because of a tremendous amount of snowfall the previous winter, the rapids were rushing at a category 5 all the way down. While on the rapids, a double wave hit. The second one knocked Michael out of the boat. The wave forced him into the water and he was carried down the rapids to his death. His body had to be airlifted out by helicopter.

John and I had gone out to dinner that night to celebrate our wedding anniversary. We came home to a life shattering telephone call.

The devastation was incomprehensible. I did not see how I could go on living. I have two other children, Matthew and Elizabeth, who I deeply love but somehow that love was separate from Michael's death.

My world, in an instant, had turned upside down and unrecognizable. I didn't know how to navigate this awful new space without my son. Meaning seemed impossible to come by. When, slowly, finally, I started to get a grip on my new reality, running gave me a sense of solidity - a goal to work toward. I decided to try to qualify for the Boston Marathon. I accomplished my goal by the skin of my teeth. I did run Boston but had a pretty poor showing. It left me wanting more.

Darren continued to encourage me to run and suggested I try a timed ultra, specifically 24 Hours Around the Lake in MA. Because I knew I would only get slower as I aged, I decided doing this 24 hour was a goal to work toward, always moving forward, never looking back. I made the decision to run this race as a fundraiser for The Liberty Humane Society in Michael's memory. Animals had always naturally taken to Michael and he had an amazing rapport with them. I wanted to connect the horrific tragedy of Michael's death with something positive. I wanted to be able to think about the animals Michael helped even after his death. The donations continued to accumulate and about $5,000 was collected and went toward improving the welfare of animals in Michael's name. I completed 60 miles in my first ultra and I felt like Michael had not only contributed to the welfare of animals but I felt like I had given a gift to Michael.

Several years ago my dear friend, Judy Quinti, and I took a hiking trip to the village of Supai on the Havasupi Indian Reservation in Arizona. Judy encouraged me to spread some of Michael's ashes there. I climbed down the canyon wall and spread some of Michael's ashes near the waterfall, Mother of All Waters. It was an incredibly beautiful place. I thought Michael would like that.

I am 72 years old now an am still running, although my speed and endurance have diminished. I have to give a shout out to Sean Gavor, aka ShamBab, for believing in me and encouraging me to move forward. In the beginning, I ran to run away from my pain. It is impossible of course, but there is physical pain in long distance running that does numb the emotional pain. It neutralizes it temporarily. I continue to run for myself.

I cannot afford to run many races but I am okay with that. I'm okay with doing miles and miles on my own because it gives me much needed peace of mind. I will continue to run for as long as I can. I am indebted to running for giving me back my life, for awarding me the ability to take control of it. I now have learned one cannot run away from one's pain but I have come to realize that pain is a part of who I am and I always carry it with me. A piece of my heart was ripped out of me when Michael died, but running has given me strength and joy to keep on going. Also, runners are a wonderful and supportive group of people. They make me laugh. I love them.

To Find What Waits
dr. lisa butler

We do not know
what we will find
down the road
off the beaten path
or under the rotting leaves
in the back yard

We run toward it
each expecting
something different

I run
mostly because it is easy
but some days I run
because it is hard

One foot
in front of the other
Simplicity itself
Meditative
Decades of repetition

These stones I carry
chafe and grind me smooth
My edges
have all gone round
and round again

It is important
to run
to find what waits
Some days it is
the edge of another stone
some days it is
more complicated

Today
I run to find simplicity itself
but do not expect it to be waiting
and I wonder
if I run long enough
could I wear away the stones

or leave them somewhere
off the beaten path.

Ed Taylor Called Me Today
dallas smith

Ed Taylor called me today. Which is odd. I was thinking about him. My wife took the call. At the time, I was running home from leaving my truck at the body shop for repair. I dented a fender and broke a light two weeks ago driving off-road through ice and snow to get to the Cummins Falls Marathon. That's where I'd met Ed, at the race. Other than that brief meeting, I didn't know him.

Everyone who runs a marathon has a story to tell. Some deserve highlighting. I'd been thinking Ed's did.

I met Ed in the heated tent before the Cummins race. I remembered him for three reasons: he's an old timer like me, so I noticed him. He was wearing a Patagonia rain jacket like the one I had on and was planning to run in - before I ditched my run. The third thing was a thought I had. I knew the weather was going to be hard on him. Conditions were the most miserable I'd ever seen, with cold rain falling and ankle-deep slush. When you're old you can't take the foul weather like a young person. I hoped Ed would be okay.

After that brief chat, I left Ed, abandoned my plans to run, and went to work on marking the course.

A few hours later I saw Ed again, at the top of Chaffin Hill, near mile 18, where I was waiting to give marathoners food and chocolate milk. His hands were cold. He'd cast off his gloves at an aid station after they'd gotten soaked. It was tough. He got in my truck and warmed his hands. I turned the heater on high and he held his hands on the dash vents. Then he took a chocolate milk and trudged on.

I returned Ed's call today and we relived those moments. He told me how happy he was to finish Cummins. And I learned a bit about his background.

He lives in Milan, in West Tennessee, the hometown he'd retired to. He and his wife moved there to be near their aging parents. He'd lived in Louisiana for thirty years, retiring a year ago as the human resources officer of an electrical distribution company. Milan is warmer, the weather less severe, than Cookeville. He'd left that fair place to come up here for the Cummins marathon during our worst ice storm. It must have been a shock.

He's had some ultramarathon experience, finishing a couple of 50K races. And the first week in May he's heading to Kirtland, OH for the Outrun 24-Hour Race. He hopes to run 50 miles in that event, a distance he has not attempted before.

At the age of 65, Ed is still stretching out, finding new challenges. He was the oldest runner to finish the Cummins Falls Marathon, posting a time of 6:24:02. Challenge met.

At the race that day, I last saw Ed when he was making the final turn, re-entering the park. I stopped to yell encouragement.

"You got this, Ed! Just four tenths more!"

He seemed buoyed by the four tenths and smiled back.

"Four tenths, huh?"

"Yep, you're nearly there."

He was. The course is a monster and the weather was a mess, but he finished. "I like to finish what I start," he told me today. And so he did.

Laces and Will... Poetry for Spring
dr. lisa butler

I waited
With the patience of a glacier
Or perhaps
The sloth of a slumbering bear
For the sun
To bring life to my trails
I researched minimalist running
In more ways than one
And dreamt of sliding over rocks
With the new found grace of spring

Blossoms bounding from buds
Leaves reaching out
Like my stride
Snowmelt uncovering ground
My feet covering ground
Tomato starts
Race starts
Endorphins start
to thaw and flow

Winter sublimates into
spring pours
into the heat of summer
Annealing sinew and bone
Coursing over gravel
And stone
With the expectancy
Of sun rise
And moon
setting fire to spirit

Laces and will
Propel me from solace
to eclipse the moment
with chase
making fast friends
with unruly shadows
and the raucous mirth
of summer

The Space Between Life and Death
kimberly durst

In the space between life and death, we're met with what we've been. We meet that person only when we're faced with being human no longer. And, it makes us feel alive.

After 180 miles, Ben Brucker was down by 7 miles. When I caught up to him, he was despondent and slow, and told me he didn't have it in him to go faster. This walk-- this was it. It wasn't getting any better than this. I paused, eyeing him in a moment that was as knowingly sad as it was curious with hope.

"You're only 7 miles back," I told him. He didn't look up. "... from 1st place."

"What?" he asked, in about as much shocked disbelief as I'd ever seen on a human. Earlier he'd been nearly 20 miles behind Tim Crow, and had spent the entire afternoon avoiding the 90 degree heat in a hotel room. He'd made an early go at it, but the hours and miles had rendered him defeated and depleted, and now, in the middle of the night, he had no more desire to run.

"Tim had some problems and he's done," I told him, "and the leaders are walking. You're 3.5 miles behind Tim Adkins." Ben ate a cereal bar standing beside my car, staring at the road ahead, no more or less quiet than usual; he's a quiet entity.

Tim was in full battle regalia, miles ahead. But, he was also exhausted, collapsed in the back of his crew SUV, trying to make nickels and dimes of what was left-- until I told him he was being chased. "How close IS that dude?" Out swung the trekking poles. Tim was on his feet. And, so they went.

And, so went the miles.

Ben called me less than 2 miles from the finish. He'd been running. Tim had been running. They'd passed John Nakel, and now were within a half mile of each other, but Ben hadn't seen Tim. I felt sorry for Ben, having given him hope, knowing that at this point he had no chance at catching Tim.

"If you run as fast as you can, you can catch him," I said. I knew it wasn't likely going to happen.

You can imagine my shock seeing them sprint down the descent into Walnut Beach, through the lot, across the boardwalk-- neck to neck after 203 miles. Into the water they splashed, and then swung their arms around each other.

Tim Adkins won the chase and the race for 2nd place

...by 1 second.

And the winner? It was a woman: Rebecca Gartrell. Don't tell me you can't. Don't tell me it can't be done.

Never give up.

The End of Something
dallas smith

It is eighty miles from my home to Nashville. Give or take a few miles. It depends on where in town you are going. Yesterday I was going to Titan's Stadium, the place where most Country Music Marathon runners park.

I got up at 3:30 a.m. and drove I-40 blurry-eyed. Once parked, I headed across the Shelby Street Pedestrian Bridge, joining a stream of runners. A slate gray morning light that earlier had hit the downtown towers now turned red. I hoped to meet a Twitter pal I've never seen. For a meeting, I'd suggested six o'clock at the foot of the bridge on Third Avenue. That wasn't a good place for her and she'd sent me a message she'd be in Corral 29 and would look for me. Good thing because the trouble I'd had getting off the Interstate and parking had eaten up forty minutes. I was too late for a six o'clock meeting anyway.

I was assigned Corral 6. Always before I'd started from Corral 1 so as to lower the gun time used in state records. This year it didn't matter. Even though I wore a marathon bib number, I intended to run the half marathon. And I intended to run it slow. State record was a non-factor.

Intended to run slow because I can't run fast. I have Graves' Disease and have had it since last Fall. It has many astonishing effects. It can cause heart disease. So they put a stent in my ticker four weeks ago. Graves' also eats your thigh muscles, among other valuable muscles. Can't run fast without thigh muscles.

Intended to run the half because on Monday I'd run the Boston Marathon, and by some miracle actually finished it, although I'd not run much prior in a couple of months. So wasn't going to run 26.2 again so soon.

Since I planned to go slow anyway, I headed to Corral 29 to look for the woman I call CT, not knowing her name. We follow each other on Twitter but have never met. She is a political wife and so keeps her identity secret. I stood in that desultory corral surrounded mostly by women and a smattering of old men, back of the pack folks for whom a half marathon is a great big deal. But I couldn't see CT. Maybe she'd show later. I drifted down to Corral 28 and looked around there, too, since I wasn't sure where one corral ended and the other began.

I could start from back here if I wanted to. It'd be different from Corral 1. It didn't matter. Time drifted on as it always does. CT didn't show and eventually we heard the race start. Nothing at all happened where we were, up on the hill at Eighth Avenue, three blocks from the starting line at Fifth.

Those starting runners headed east down Broad, turned south on First, and west on Demonbreun. They finally hit Broad and ran right past where we stood. I saw last year's marathon winner Scott Wietecha in front, Brian Shelton on his shoulder. Brian, from my town, is running well these days. I thought he might win the half.

CT didn't show, and I figured at this point she wouldn't. But I couldn't stop looking for her. Later I saw where she'd sent me a direct message on Twitter that she'd been bumped to Corral 15. I'd failed to see that message and didn't now have my phone.

Nothing much happened, except occasionally we'd drift a few steps down the hill toward the starting line, still nearly three blocks away. Twice they moved the corral ropes toward Fifth, and we'd advance thirty yards or so before standing around again.

Running a half marathon slowly is just a typical morning run for me, no great challenge. Just a matter of putting in time. We stood around. Eventually we'd get our chance. No hurry.

I had a streak going. I was one of the thirty-eight "Fifteen Year Runners." We'd run all previous editions of the race. As a reward, they'd given us comp entry and a special vanity bib to wear, one colored black, a different color from the 30,000 other bibs. That was sure to bring shout-outs from fans. At the moment, mine was hidden under a throw-away tee.

This race holds the story of my running. Our histories entwine. I ran the very first one just one year after my first marathon, just two years after my first race of any length. My running grew up with this race. In that first one, which came just twelve days after Boston, I ran ten minutes faster than I'd ever run.

For each of the first six races, 2000 through 2005, I ran personal records on this hilly course, even though I was running lots of other races on flatter courses that you'd figured I would run faster than here. This was a lucky race for me. I set eight age-group records here. And I won my age division an unlikely twelve consecutive times, beating the great Ken Brewer once by just forty-five seconds.

As I stood waiting in Corral 29 with my vanity bib hidden, I knew no marathon record was in play today. In fact I'd be running not the marathon but the half marathon. Not even running it. Only jogging.

We stood and waited. We moved forward again a few yards. Then I walked away.

I stepped out of the corral and walked down the hill toward the starting line, skipping up on the sidewalk to dodge spectators. Around Corral 15, I cut through the shuffling stream and emerged on the other side of Broad, just above Bridgestone Arena.

I walked beside Bridgestone to Demonbreun and paused, watching runners stream up the hill. I headed on down to Fourth and turned up toward Broad to Schermerhorn Symphony Center, where I cut over to the Shelby Street Pedestrian Bridge.

Fans leaning over the rail above First Avenue were watching the south-streaming marathoners below. Fans and runners alike whooped and called out. I stood and watched a few minutes. The stream would diminish to a trickle before another wave emerged. We couldn't see them coming down Broad until they turned the corner at a red brick building onto First. Suddenly a colorful mass flowed, surging around the corner.

I walked on across the bridge toward the Titan's parking lot, meeting hollow-eyed runners wearing bibs, who'd arrived too late to run, probably beginners who didn't know one had to arrive early for such a race. They all had numbers in the 20-or-30 thousand range. My number, still hidden under the tee, read 435.

At the car I changed clothes, putting on the blue Boston finisher's tee I earned on Monday. I could go down to the finish line area, stand around watching runners come in. I'll have friends there. The shirt would be a conversation starter. But I realized that, by now, the winner of the half would have already finished. Brian Shelton, I would learn, finished in fourth place. Scott Wietecha would go on to win the marathon.

I decided against the finish line. I wanted to be through with this place. I grabbed my phone and saw where CT had sent me the change-of-plans message I'd never seen.

Throw it all away. The comp entry, the vanity bib, the annual tradition, the streak, the history - everything. Throw it away. I put up a tweet:

"Did not start, am not sorry, do not care. Am I being clear? #DNS #CMM"

Then I cranked up and drove away. But I don't know. It could be a lie, my tweet. I don't know.

April Fifteenth
dallas smith

Six Years After

A yellow long-sleeved tee and not just any yellow tee but rather a Boston Marathon finisher's tee and more specifically than that a Boston finisher's tee carrying in large print running down the sleeve the message "2013," that was what I wore on my 20-mile training run this morning, a run in solidarity with all my brothers and sisters running the Boston Marathon today and remembering what happened there on this date six years ago.

Day Of

I remember it too well. I managed to take third place in my age group but almost lost the whole deal due to mounting blindness on the course (a history of extraordinary eye trauma and some dozen surgeries is part of my story). I could see blurred images of large objects but no detail, like looking through the shower curtain. I retained enough vision to find the finish line and then melted into the stirring crowd of recovering runners while my vision continued to decline.

Finally a young volunteer, a sophomore at Boston University, took me by the hand. She was leading me through the crowd when the bombs exploded. All became confusion and chaos, ambulances, police cars, and military vehicles pushing through the parting throng. But the sophomore didn't leave me until we arrived at a safe place where my daughter Jill was waiting. Jill, I learned, had not left the finish area until two minutes before the blast, narrowly avoiding a close call.

The whole long story of all that happened to me that day is much too lengthy to lay out here—and maybe I never will. Over the years, I've been reluctant to talk about it; my story, no matter how poignant it might be to me, stands ultimately trivial beside that of the people hit and injured or killed. I don't want my story to detract from theirs.

That day, I ran right past the bomb, as thousands of others did. There is no reason explaining why some were stricken while others passed safely on. In our utter helplessness and inability to understand the tragedy's selection we give it a name and call the name "fate." That's all mortals can do.

And we remember.

Day After

On the day after the Boston Marathon bombing of April 15, 2013, Anita and Lynn Burnett walked up to our hotel to visit with my daughter Jill and me. Their hotel and ours were both within the secured area soldiers had established immediately after the blast. That area encompassed several blocks downtown, enclosing office buildings, restaurants, hotels, and the Prudential Center, a high-rise shopping center.

Overnight, my degraded vision had returned to normal. Meanwhile, Lynn had become a celebrity. A Nashville TV station, realizing a local Tennessee runner had finished barely before the blast, called him up and interviewed him on-air. Following that, his Facebook page flooded with friend requests.

We decided to take a walk outside the secured area and went through a checkpoint just outside our hotel that was manned by soldiers carrying M-16s. The soldiers requested proof in the form of room keys that we were duly lodged in the hotel. We didn't have a room key. Jill and I had just checked out because we were heading back to Tennessee later in the day. We had stored our luggage there to pick up later, and I had the hotel receipt for it. The soldiers inspected the paper and let us pass. It likely didn't hurt that Lynn and I, two beanstalk-slender runners, were wearing our Boston Marathon jackets.

We walked along in the Back Bay area, a neighborhood of

neatly kept row houses and brownstones. It was like a quiet Sunday morning, peaceful, and idyllic. But you could see barriers across the streets leading downtown where the bombing had happened the day before.

We drifted along. The walk was good and what Lynn and I needed to help our legs recover. Suddenly a young woman came out of a house. She'd seen our jackets. She walked up to Lynn and me and handed each of us a long-stemmed red rose.

"I want to thank you for coming to Boston to run the marathon," she said.

Despite what you may've heard about the gruff temperament of Bostonians, the woman's act was in total keeping with the kindness extended to me by Boston residents over the years during my trips there.

We walked on, Lynn and I clutching our roses, touched by the woman's kind gesture. After a while, we came to a side street barricade, manned by two soldiers. I walked up to the barricade and reached my rose across it to one of the soldiers, saying,

"A woman gave me this rose and thanked me for coming and running the marathon. I want to give it to you now to thank you for your service."

The young soldier accepted the rose with a smile. Following my lead, Lynn gave his rose to the second soldier. We walked on, leaving the two soldiers standing behind the barrier holding their roses and their rifles.

I don't know; memory can play tricks, it can be wrong. It's a patchwork of images, sounds, and scenes, of things said and not said. It is plastic and can be molded by later events and the passage of time.

Nonetheless, the enduring image I hold onto is that of the two soldiers standing there holding their roses and rifles. We four walked on and passed out of that scene and out of that story, and came back to our lives in Tennessee.

The families ripped apart by the cruel blasts that day can never walk out of that scene, out of that story. Time stopped. For them, it is forever yesterday.

I Was Not Expecting the Mist

amy mower

I was not expecting the mist.

Suspended droplets
sucking the glow
of my headlamp
caging the light
until it is a cocoon
swaddling me in
an envelope of uncertainty
not knowing
not seeing
hiding the ups
and the downs
of the trail
every step
a step
into the unknown.

I was not expecting the mist.

My muffled footfalls
punch through this cloud
for the briefest of moments
I shape the chaos with
rhythm and purpose

Droplets coalesce and
capture my spirit
they shimmer with my electric glow

Briefly (briefly!)
I am
solid

though after my passing
the droplets regather
and entropy reigns
once more

Formless disarray
it could have been binding
Instead it unveiled possibilities

Ghostly tendrils of insight
and freedom
caressing my face
like tears

Those journeys where the way seems plain
are the real illusion ...
headlamp blazing
a cone of safety
crystal clear nights
beckon "Come hither"
I think I see everything
and just like that
catch my foot on a root
and go sprawling

Be wary when the path seems clear
Head bravely into the mist.
It is in the losing that we find our way.

I was not expecting the mist.

The Invisible Woman
alene nitzky

When I first started running ultras in the early 1990s, there weren't a lot of other women in the sport. At every race, the field was overwhelmingly male. Women were only a curiosity if not an afterthought; some of the older men marveled at our participation, as if it were an aberration of human nature.

We weren't exactly treated like Jock Semple treated Kathrine Switzer at the 1967 Boston Marathon, but for all purposes, we were oddities--baby nurturing machines out there perspiring—because, as my generation was told growing up, girls don't sweat. Most of the time, it was like no one even *saw* us, let alone acknowledging our existence or stopping to get to know us.

If I wanted training partners, they had to be men, because where I lived, I was the only woman I was aware of who was running ultras at the time. Luckily for me, I had no trouble keeping up with my male counterparts.

Before I ever ran my first ultra, I discovered I had a gift of speed that allowed me to excel in distance running. I pushed myself to discover my limits and found my breaking point quickly. After spending more downtime with injuries than actual training and running, I finally realized speed might not be such a worthy goal if I wanted to keep running.

I met a small group of ultrarunners in my hometown, all men, and began running with them. I soon discovered how much I loved ultras- the freedom of being out all day on the trails outdoors, the scenery, and the challenges of climbing and descending, with the views and exertion as rewards. The camaraderie of getting to know each other as we spent hours together on a weekly basis covering dozens of miles was also worthwhile, as these developed into long lasting friendships.

My gift seemed to advantage me in ultras on the roads and track, but not so much on the trails. I loved training on the track for pure speed, and I viewed the trail runs as icing on the cake of enjoyment. I won or placed high in almost every race I ran that wasn't on a trail.

Women who won ultras were barely noticed though, compared to men. Mentioning the top women runners was an afterthought; sometimes we went completely unmentioned in race reports, written, of course, by men. Nobody seemed to care or pay much attention to the women's competition except for the women runners ourselves.

There was a certain safety in invisibility, though, because when you went to a race, nobody knew who you were, ever heard of you, or cared. There was little pressure or hype during pre-race dinners or briefings. You could train on the race course and nobody you encountered would know you by name. At the race, you could just melt into the crowd. "Go First Woman!" was yelled out in a solitary female voice somewhere along the sidelines as you came into an aid station. I'd always smile to myself, though, that *someone* was paying attention.

Over the years that followed, more women began to enter the sport, top women gained recognition and acceptance, and records fell. Eventually you could count on there being a real race among the women's field, and more often women began to win races outright against the men. At first it was major news when a woman beat all the men in the field; eventually it became less of a surprise. More men acknowledged the existence and competitive credentials of women, and the additional publicity contributed to more voices along the sidelines cheering for us. Women began to receive more sponsorships, interviews, and placement in sports reporting, but it is still far from equal to men, even though women regularly make up half the field or close to it at many ultra events.

In life, as well as sport, women are much less visible in most arenas, except when it comes to looks and physical attributes. I see it in the supermarket, the young guy stocking the shelves goes right up to the woman half my age to ask her if she's finding everything okay, but completely ignores me, standing an equal distance away, obviously struggling to find an item. The right body type, face, provocative clothes and makeup, being the girlfriend or wife or trophy, and demeanor, is still expected, complete with a smile and acceptance of whatever is given to us, and never demanding more. In a world created by and for men first, it is a slow process of change to admit, accept, elevate and promote women, much less see and regard us as people who are equals, regardless of the institution we are talking about.

The gift of aging brings less care about what other people think, how we should look, or caring about pleasing others. Everything we do is for a purpose. If we don't enjoy it, we're much less likely to agree to it. We start to realize that time is short, we need to make the most of what we've got left, and worrying about what other people think of us or how they see us is a waste of effort and time.

As we age, with life in general as well as running specifically, we become invisible once again. The invisibility of older women is a blessing in some ways; we can do our work without anyone really paying attention to us, so we can work efficiently and effectively without the distractions of men butting in, clumsily neglecting to read the room, changing the topic, mansplaining, or talking over us. We can get the job done with the satisfaction of knowing we accomplished it, without needing the attention or accolades a younger person might want.

We don't have to prove anything- we *are* the proof. We overcame all the obstacles and being ignored and disregarded, and here we are, still going, still doing what we love, never having let all that stop us. In our invisibility, we have become more visible to ourselves. We can see in clear relief against the dull backdrop of the same old scripts, how colorful and unique and valuable we are, without needing anyone to acknowledge us for it. We shine brightly, even if we are invisible to others. It's not that they can't see us, it's that they choose not to. They miss out on the wisdom and stories and history and lessons we bring to the table.

While I've often cherished the anonymity and invisibility, there were also times when I felt that I had something to contribute and the value of what I had to say was completely disregarded or ignored, or never even given a chance to speak up unless I asserted myself forcefully with a demand. These days I still see some of the men who offer to coach women overlooking certain physiologic truths and needs that we have, as if women have nothing to offer each other.

On the streets where I used to get leers or catcalls while running, now I get a thumbs up, which is quite a welcome change, though there is something subtly denigrating about that behavior, as if the viewer doesn't believe their eyes.

As I've evolved as a runner myself, I no longer feel compelled to perform or even train to do my best. I choose events based on their uniqueness, scenery, the trip that accompanies them, the other people I might encounter at the race, or along the way. I run the event in order to enrich my life experience, or restore my psyche, or to feel surrounded by an odd sort of family I've come to know over decades.

I feel that I am on a life cycle: when I first started running, I too was amazed at the oldest runners and how they persisted in ultras, often multiday events, without fading. Later I came to know many of them, watching them enjoy running into their oldest and final years. I've said goodbye to many of them unknowingly that it would be the final time I'd see them run.

And now I am in the process of taking their place. I am now one of the older runners, though not the oldest yet. I hope I will be able to take their place as I run out my years to the end of my life. I hope some younger runner I've inspired will someday have a chance to see me in my last run, allowing me to pay it forward.

As we age, we begin to understand the great value within and among ourselves. We've learned to make our own fun, create our own experiences, tell our own rich and precious stories. You won't read about them in the pages of the magazines, you won't see us in product advertising, and you won't see us standing by as the trophy of some wiry thirty-something bearded mountain goat at the top of the podium.

So the next time you, regardless of your gender, see a group of gray haired women huddled together laughing after a run, or running together on the trails, think about us as a mine of diamonds, gems whose wealth you will only get to share if you are willing to dig down deep into the pile of treasures, first by seeing, then acknowledging, listening, and learning. And if you do, you will be warmly welcomed.

Sisyphe, saxo
adrian gentry

Cap stones five times round.
The sacrifice does dream so.
No. Taps you nitwit.

Running

bonnie muetterties

It calls me.
Motion, effort, it starts with a wink.
It draws me to itself
And then in a blink,
It caresses me
and holds me tight.
We spend hours together, day and night.
We are not alone.
It seeks us all.
We gather together and respond to its call.
Its hows and whys
Its ups and downs,
It feeds us and takes us down to the ground.
We listen and learn and try to respond,
Again and again
so closely we bond.
The friends and the love it brings on its way,
The inner strength that blesses our day.
It calls me.
Is it a sprint or an ultra,
Is it trail or on road?
What is it we're chasing,
or is it all code?
Our passion for freedom, justice and fame?
To remind us to try, to explore and remain?
To be true to ourselves
And never give up?
Get set!
We're more than the podiums we'll never get,
and yet?
It calls me.

Savor The Moment
fred murolo

All right, I'll say it. I loved Stu. Loved him. From the moment I met him, he proved to be a character. But he was also generous and kind and good-hearted. I like to think I got what he was talking about, but his inner monologue was probably something to the effect that he was surrounded by idiots and Murolo just couldn't keep up.

At Volstate 2011, Joe Judd and I find ourselves walking along the road from the ferry to the overlook in Hickman when this man walks up alongside. He has the shortest shorts and the whitest skinny legs. He opens with a story about being able to do a quarter mile in under 50 seconds back in his youth. Joe suggests he bust one out right now. This is Stu. Later in the race, after he has dropped, he and Marv meet us, walking together again, as if we had the whole way, and he insists we drink a coke. He tells us the best ultra beverage is coke mixed with milk.

And we became friends. I'm sure not as close as many on the list, but friends. We spent a lot of time walking at Ancient Oaks the last 5 years, and exchanged stories, and I heard many of his. About the years associated with NASA (but don't call him a rocket scientist; he had no use for those fuckers). About the blond disaster, the convertible with the bullet holes, the cats, Kissimmee, relationships coming and going. The prospect of dying. Cancer and chemo ("weedkiller"). We talked a lot.

And I was at the pasta meal before Ancient Oaks in 2014, when Stu picked up the check for about 10 of us because he thought it was a hassle to split those things with so many people. I had dinner with him again last year the night before the race, but didn't run with him as much because I was going for a faster time. I wish I had walked a whole lap or more with him.

In the middle of the night on the Ancient Oaks course in 2015, while running alone, my headlamp illuminated a tall man walking with a hatchet in hand. Then as I approached from behind he dropped to a knee and started chopping at a root that no doubt had pissed him off for the last time. Stu.

I think the best way I can describe Stu is that he can discuss quantum theory with ease while at the same time saying Schrodinger was a fuck for using a cat in his example.

Amazing brain. Amazing guy. The world is a little more drab today. I miss him already.

Fred in CT

(yeah, I teared up when I heard the news and when I read Carl's post and Pat's post)

Goobers

dallas smith

Six miles into a run in a rural county where dogs run wild and people do too, I was hiking up a long hill while I ate a pack of M&Ms. During the first four miles, it had rained hard and steady. I was still soggy and waterlogged.

I finished the snack and was rolling up the empty pack to stuff in my shorts pocket. Just then a beat up old pickup rolled up from behind and stopped. A kindly old gent with a beard like a white broom looked over.

"You need a lift?"

"No, thanks, I'm training."

It was as if I'd said the most ordinary thing you could possibly hear on this country road. Without another word, the man reached across the seat and lifted up a two-pound plastic jar of honey-roasted peanuts, still about half full.

"Hold your hand," said he.

He filled my hand and was still pouring. Peanuts were falling on the road.

"Hold your other hand," he said.

I cupped my hands together and he poured out a giant pile of peanut, until peanuts were sliding down the slope and falling on the pavement.

"That'll help you," he said, and began to rumble away.

"Thank you, I love peanuts," I shouted as he pulled away.

I stood on the wet pavement cradling the pile of peanuts. Trees overhead were dripping. The truck passed out of hearing.

What to do with the peanuts? I hate to waste food. I'd planned my snacks to simulate the race I was training for, and stuffed the snacks in the pockets of my shorts. I'd brought two packs of M&Ms, a pack of peanut M&Ms and a Pay Day bar. I'd just finished the first pack of M&Ms.

I'd accepted the peanuts from the man. That was the right thing to do. It is a kindness to accept help when people offer. It gives them pleasure and satisfaction.

The clock was running and I stood in indecision. Finally I leaned my face down to the pile and began chomping peanuts, like a pig eating corn in a trough. More peanuts fell to the pavement. Birds will follow me after this, I thought. Eventually I ate enough to free up one hand, but I still held a handful of honey-roasted peanuts.

What now? I noticed the empty M&M pack folded between my fingers. I'd never gotten around to stowing it. It'd be like stuffing toothpaste back into the tube. I decided to try, and started funneling peanuts into the wet pack. The side seams were beginning to come unglued. More peanuts fell to the pavement. Eventually I ended up with a lemon-sized lump of peanuts bound more or less by paper, and I stuffed the lump into an empty pocket.

The lump stayed there until I finished my 24-mile run. Then it became my recovery snack. I dug it out and ate those last peanuts as I walked back up to the house. A few more fell on the ground.

High Mileage Experiment Second Report
fred murolo

For love of the game.

I loved Laz's free verse poetry about running and running on into "maturity." I've been kicking it around in my mind since he published it. Now, Laz is certainly erudite-er than I, but please let me share a little running love.

As a few of you know, I have been on a long higher mileage experiment. It started with the goal of laying down at least 20,000 steps every day. It grew into a combination of running and walking with a GPS watch this year, doing as many miles as my body can comfortably handle. As of this writing I am at 5,270 miles for the year. This is a snapshot of how I got here.

I should premise this by saying the experiment starts with an overwhelming love of running. I wake up every morning thinking of the day as a blank canvas ready to be run on. At the end of each month, when I tally my miles, I think "Excellent, tomorrow I get to start at zero and do it again."

Tuesday, November 21: It's the Tuesday before Thanksgiving, and I don't have anything pressing in the office this morning. My wife is going to the gym, so no run-walk with her, just a morning run. I am up at 5:45, and it's dark. I put on running clothes—a base layer, then light wind pants and a hoodie, for 32-degree weather. I lace up Hoka Stinson 3 ATRs. I have a cup of tea, use the bathroom. I make espresso for later. I bring the trash out to the garage. My wife gets up and puts out my son's breakfast. My son gets up for high school. I wish him a good day. I head out the door at 6:40, down Cherry Street, right at the stop sign and down the hill to the linear park, a paved rail trail. It's just getting full light. I pass the fast-walking old guy outbound. He's a regular—cursory wave. So too, the guy who walks with the golf club. He always says good morning. I pass the mile mark. The watch buzzes and reads 10:30. I usually start slow, to work out yesterday's stiffness. I pass

178

the guy with the white hair. He nods.

Fast-walking woman and her friend and dog are coming at me. We say hi, and they're gone in a flash. She really hauls. Then I'm across Higgins Road and on to the 2-mile mark. Second mile is 9:30; I'm warming up. Then I'm across North Brooksvale and going past the old canal lock. (The canal was built in the 1820s to haul goods between New Haven and Northampton, Mass., back when the Northeast was a manufacturing powerhouse. Then, in the 1840s, the railroad followed the path of the canal and put it out of business. Then the railroad closed down and left us the linear park.) I see the ladies who walk down on this section. They have matching sweatshirts that say "The Posse." One of them is a client. They all say good morning as we pass. I hit the 3-mile mark. That mile is 9:22. I calculate my time. I turn at the bridge at 3.4, so I can make it back to my daughter's bus stop for 7:44. I speed it up a little going Northbound, passing the ladies, who say in unison, "Have a nice day," passing the woman with the skinny dog with a coat and the guy who always wears shorts and looks like Santa. We exchange a "Morning." His dog doesn't seem to like me. As I pass, he sometimes leaps at me with a bark. His human knows to hold tight to the leash. I pass the old couple that never makes eye contact or talks and their little dog. I pass the kid (early 20s?), who runs on the grass beside the trail. He wears a Towson State hoodie; he never says hi either. Miles 4, 5 and 6 are 9:15 or a little faster. I pass the Chevy Volt guy. We nod; we used to have something in common. I wave to the crossing guard; her daughter is in the marching band with my son. I chug up the hill to the bus stop and see my daughter. We usually talk for about a minute in the morning before her bus comes. I make some dumb dad puns; she complains about the cold or the upcoming school day. Today, the bus comes after about 30 seconds. I tell her I love her and wish her a good day. I'm at 6.8 miles.

If my wife were not going to the gym, I would go back to the house and we would do a 4-mile run-walk, but I'm on my own today. It's warming up and it's a pleasant morning. I run up West Main past the coffee shop and the convenience store, onto Main Street past the Catholic church, the law firm, the spa, past a few old homes, past

179

the little cemetery, down to South Main. I go past the Episcopal Church and the old school my mother went to in the 1930s. I'm just cruising along. I figure I'll do about 11 miles. I take a right and go down the dead-end street the Senator lives on. I come back out and go down another dead end. I go back around to Main Street toward the library and go right again this time staying on South Main to the Town Green. I'm at about 8 miles. I take a right on Cornwall and head back toward the linear park. I go left and make a little circle past our US Representative's house, then back onto Cornwall down the hill some. I pass my daughter's friend's parents running on their way back from the trail. If I turned around for home right now, it would be about 10 miles. I'm thinking 11. And then I get onto the park trail and I just glide down the same paved course I just did earlier. My pace picks up a bit. Karen won't be at the office till 10:15. Nothing is urgent; I have plenty of time. If I turn here, I'll have 11. It passes. Here would be 12. That passes too. 13?

No. Then I'm past this morning's turnaround and I head into Hamden, the town to the South. I turn back under the powerlines, thinking 17. I haul it back. The miles are holding in the mid-9's. I get to the end of the linear park and head straight into the vet's long driveway, then up and back on Laurel Lane, then down Sheila Lane, the short cul-de-sac. I add in a few tenths on Spring Street. It's starting to look like 18. And then I go past the driveway and back past like I'm circling the drain and then I'm home.

18.2 miles, 2:56.

It's 9:36, just enough time to drink my espresso and a smoothie, shower and dress and make it to work before my wife walks in. I'm feeling a little ragged, right hammy a little sore, but I am working at my desk, when she walks in.

"Hi Honey. Anything going on?"

"Hi. Not much."

How was your run?"

"Great."

Two Bridge Crossings

amy mower

Two bridge crossings
both dark
the first so early I'm pretty sure
I'm the only one out there that has already gone to bed
and slept 7 hours
just me, the homeless, and the
occasional student

It's a different sort of quiet
seedy
edgy
full of promise
and a little danger
or maybe a lot

Last stretch of city before the trail
lights like Christmas
brilliantly battle the velvet dark
twinkling lights smear and glisten
on the water below, inky black,
quiet and beckoning
I hear whispering from the depths

100 feet and I'm over the bridge
I hit the trail at the Wall of Death
mile 3.7
It's me and the trail for the next 11

Hours later, crossing back it
looks the same
still dark
still inky
difference is
I'm no longer alone

thin boats with green lights
cut through the water
rhythmically
the oarsmen rowing
in unison
pull under the bridge
just as I cross

This way is downhill
And I am flying with gravity
and the knowledge that
I am almost done,
drunk from the heady perfume
of butter wafting from the
French bakery

And while I've been out here
morning has come ...
This miracle propels me up the hill
(which is mighty)
and home to a day
that now might be considered
close to normal

Running Memories
kimberly durst

"What are your favorite running memories from the decade?"

Idk. I've been there and done that. Photos and words can't tell the stories quite like the achy bones, scars, traumas and joy.

Some of the best memories aren't attached to awards or accolades, and I don't have any photographic evidence they ever happened.

Ten years? That's 5,258,880 minutes. I don't know how many of them were spent running, how many more spent thinking about it.

People obsess over things celebrity, and even in a niche sport like ultra running, that obsession exists. I gravitate away from the big name events, although I've run every Lazarus Lake race except Big's, with an interesting spectrum of results. On the one hand, I have 2 of the fastest screwed women's Vol States in history. On the other hand, I have the slowest complete Barkley Marathons loop ever recorded, and the event has been held for over 35 years.

I started a 5k in the front row wearing a tutu and nearly blew the women's competition out of the water racing in it.

I finished dead last, 14 minutes past the cutoff in the 2015 Mohican 100.

Running is a very personal thing, and something I've enjoyed on private journeys as well as from a competitive angle for almost 25 years. Many of my dreams came to life over the past decade, from finishing my first 100 nearly 8 years ago, to living on the street out of my pack during my many journey runs.

Through running, I've met some of my best friends. The companionship I've enjoyed during some of my road journeys means more to me than any of my medals, trophies, or buckles.

I can't pick a favorite memory-- or 5. But, these are some of what made the past decade.

Cheers,
#feral

9 Haiku

bill gentry

Endurance preaches,
showing us a stark beauty
through intense failure.

Running by headlamp,
me and my rhythmic footfalls
and sweet dreams of you.

Running every day
may take a measured toll, but
oh does my soul smile.

Step by painful step
through the dense fog of fatigue,
ultrarunning's gift.

Running through Life's fog,
I feel wave after soft wave
of resounding peace.

Footfalls always match
murmurs of my hippie soul,
running cleansing me.

RUN TO SAVE YOUR LIFE

Of the profound way
running purifies my soul,
I will never tire.

It's my jam because
running unleashes my soul,
each breath a rebirth.

Come and play with me
where the trails lead to the sea,
our souls running free.

The Invisible Companion
kimberly durst

Selfish,
or misunderstood?
I hear racing, in the purest sense of the term, is a selfish endeavor.
But, I wonder...
Have you felt the wind on your back, and wondered if he felt what you were feeling?
There's a force field that bridges the gap between those two bodies.
There's an awareness-- a constant awareness-- that you're sharing a conscious pondering about any atmospheric disturbance that might shake up the next few hours. You wonder when you're going to hear footsteps and breathing. You wonder while you're eating that pickle or plum, relieving your bowels, repairing your feet.
You wonder when you're going to see him.
The pain swallows your senses, and you look over your shoulder just as the sun is beginning to rise over the tree line, and you know he's out there.
He's moving.
You're moving.
He sees the sun rising.
The world keeps breathing.
You work with each other's strengths and weaknesses.
You despair.
You smile.
You stare.
Your legs scream.
Your head pounds.
And, you know, every step of the way, that he's coming. It's an unavoidable truth, glaring in the heat and sweat. It's everywhere.
But, when it's over, win or lose, you're never the same, and you never look at each other the same way either. Staring, face to face, at that person who existed in a parallel universe for a hundred or more miles, for a blip of a moment, you're staring at your own reflection,
because you're the person to him that he was to you;

and, you've been there and done that, and he was-- in every
imaginable way, your companion.
And, there is nothing,
nothing,
selfish about that kind of shared love. You shake hands or sit side
by side, with words and with silence, and you've done something
big. He has, too.

Perhaps you'll look for a rematch,
a beer,
or no words at all for 20 years.
It doesn't really matter in the end.
It's just running.
And, it is about the journey.
But, a journey is more than footsteps and climbing up the walls of
your skull;
and the invisible companion,
is a devil, savior, and best friend
in the darkest moments on the road.

Knickers!

adrian gentry

The pages say follow the trail?
Grab a page from a book made of braille?
But my toe nails are mush
And my knickers are flush
Why chase the accursed white whale.

Mr. Competent
patrick mcHenry

I'm always filled with excitement and a little anxiety as I near the end of the drive, and the hills I'll be 'playing on' come into view. Especially so this morning, as I could see there was still a lot of snow on the ground showing through the trees. In just a few minutes I'd be making the steep climb up to the top of that ridge on the right to begin my roughly twelve-mile loop. There was rain in the forecast, and I figured I'd be the only one out here, pretty much - just the way I like it.

The trails would likely be icy - but I had on my screw shoes, so I was ready for that. Temperatures were in the upper thirties (F) - but I know how to dress for that. I was all set to add or remove layers as necessary once I got warmed up.

I thought about all this as I made my way up that first climb. The screw shoes working with not a bit of slippage on the beaten, ice-slicked trail. When I reached the first short, gentle downgrade to the stream crossing, just above the waterfall, I broke into a trot on the ice. "Just keep your center of gravity over your feet and the shoes will do the rest," I told myself confidently.

I thought about how my ten-year anniversary as an ultrarunner had quietly passed just a few months ago. Ten years ago I heard a recommendation for a book that sounded interesting, called "Born to Run: A Hidden Tribe, Super athletes, and the Greatest Race the World Has Never Seen." By the time I finished it I was an ultrarunner, if only in spirit at first (it would be over two years before I ran that first 50K at Oil Creek). I had come a long way since then, I thought, as I leaped from one shallow spot to another, crossing the creek just above the falls. I had long since learned not to try to jump onto large rocks showing above the water in situations like this. In these temperatures what looks like just a wet rock could actually be glazed with a coating of crystal-clear ice. Landing on your butt in snow run-off is a good deal less pleasant than just getting your feet wet in it.

I kind of like it that there's a stream crossing like this so early in the run. I get to suck it up and commit to dealing with wet feet right away, so I can quit worrying about it and just enjoy the rest of the day. The right socks make wet feet a non-issue on a short run like this anyway.

I really had come a long way, I thought again - to a place of smooth, casual competence to do these things - things that ninety-something percent of other fifty-eight-year-olds would never think of doing. I do mountain trail runs in winter, because I can, and because I know how to do them.

Halfway up the second part of the climb I was starting to overheat, so I stopped at a switchback to take a layer off my upper body. I found a dry spot to lay my pack, and quickly pulled off my rain shell, and then the zipper-necked pullover. As I stooped to stuff that in my pack, I thought, "Hmm... that's odd. It's already unzipped. I don't remember doing that when I took it off."

Then I noticed a bunch of my stuff was gone. "Well, Mr. Competent, nice going! Now what do you think you ought to do?" The stuff I was missing wasn't that terrible to lose. Except for the buff it was all consumable, one-time-use stuff - and the buff was pretty cheap and easy to replace.

There was honor though. "Mr. Competent" would not be leaving his stuff strewn all over the trail like a moron today! I turned around and headed back down. The biggest concern was that one of the most likely places for it all to have bounced out of there was when I was leaping the creek - and anything that fell out there would quickly have been swept right over the eighty-foot waterfall. I resolved that if necessary I'd go all the way back down and see if I could find anything swirling in an eddy below the falls. It was, after all, a matter of honor and pride.

Fortunately I found it all on the trail - after I'd crossed back over the creek. Everything had already fallen out before I'd gotten there the first time. Stuff re-acquired, and securely ZIPPED inside the pack, I crossed the creek one more time and went on my way, chagrined.

It was a murderously hard run-hike around that loop in those conditions, and I think my legs will be complaining about it quite a bit later today and tomorrow - but I did it, one more time. Here's hoping I'll still be doing it when I'm sixty-eight. Maybe then I'll really be competent at it.

Spartathlon 2019
balázs korányi

Spartathlon 2019 – 246 kilometers across Greece

I

Can you have a first love a second time? Can a magical spell lift you, shake you up, and torture you again, just like it did before? Can everything that feels familiar also be new and strange?

Running towards Sparta, I recognized every sound, smell, and scene. Yet, it felt like I'd never been there before. I was both at home and in a new, forbidden place. I recognized every turn, yet felt lost.

It's difficult to explain love. It just exists. And every adjective you use to try to explain it just weakens it because it forces you to single out individual snippets of the magic. This love is of the children lining up for autographs and cheering you on until the wee hours of the morning; it's of the tiny flickers of light from the torches along the mountainside; and it's of the villages where even the priest comes out to cheer you on. This love is of the turquoise sea, the smell of the fresh grapes in the vineyards, the late-night coffee that keeps you going, the new and old friends, the eucalyptus trees, and the relics of ancient Greece which dot the land. It includes the humbleness of ordinary people, the love they send your way, and the stray dogs that join the runners and stop for a drink at the aid stations just like the humans do. The love includes the emotional exhaustion that you manage to shake off time and again, and the physical constraints that don't really exist. And the final manifestation of that love is when you swear 'never again' as you stagger up to the statue of Leonidas, and then start making plans to run again a few days later.

That was my first love, but I lost it 11 years ago. We broke up, and I can't really explain why. Maybe the passion was too intense, and it sapped my energy. Yet ignoring it didn't work either.

It left me feeling empty inside. I was last in Sparta in 2008. Like now, I ran down Sparta's main road, touched the statue, and swore, like many times before, never to run again. Until tomorrow.

But tomorrow turned into the next day, then next week and next year. I sat on the proverbial couch with my Spartathlon medal and got stuck there. The unimaginable happened: I lost my will to run. I sat on that couch for years with a coke and bag of chips, waiting for the magic to return. The years came and went, and I stuck to my white lie that I could make a comeback anytime; after all, the Black Knight always triumphs! But as I sat, Sparta, running, and sports in general faded into a distant memory.

My 2019 Spartathlon started out on this proverbial couch. So, to me this race is only partly about running. But mostly about why you should never wait until tomorrow and why you should never stop dreaming. Without dreams, we're just droids, after all.

II

The motto of another legendary ultra race used to be: "The Barkley eats its young." The Spartathlon is even less gracious. The Spartathlon will chew you up and spit you out onto the pavement over and over again, forcing you to get up and keep moving. It makes you believe that you still have a chance, only if you dare to get up. As long as you keep going, it's not over!

This was my mantra as I was jolted awake after crashing into the dense bushes on the side of the road. It was around 1:30 a.m., not far from Kaparelli, and I guess I fell asleep walking up the hill. I fought a losing battle to keep my eyes open, but my legs kept going. It only lasted a couple of moments but was a powerful reminder that in the Spartathlon, nothing is certain and your fortunes can turn on a dime.

Still, that little accident was also one of the highlights of the day; collapse and recovery in one. Because the Spartathlon will also show you its best side during the night. Beneath the light of the Milky Way, the night and the silent mountainside were mine. I hadn't seen anybody for ages and the loneliness empowered and pushed me forward. Allons enfants de la Patrie, Marchons! Marchons!

We'd been on the road for about a day by then, but the Spartathlon's bad habit is that it takes a long time to really get underway. You need to run 90K, maybe even a 100K before you feel that you are really doing it. Exhaustions and recoveries up to that point are just tests to see whether you've done your homework, and whether you qualify to go on. Hermes will send along a string of panic attacks to test whether you know what you're doing and to expose the impostor. But this time I really did my homework, I swear, I did.

At the start, I did not meditate by the ancient wall, like I did 11 years ago; I didn't bite my nails; my stomach wasn't in knots. I didn't have any doubts. My training was complete. I'd done everything I wanted to do so there was no reason to doubt myself. I walked around, watched the clock impatiently and took selfies with my supporter, Bogi, and the rest of my crew. I didn't have anything left to do. I had run the start through my head a thousand times already. No, this race wouldn't be about luck.

The Spartathlon is more an exercise in meditation than running, I would argue. But you need a certain amount of self-confidence for this meditation to work. I won't say running is not important, but it may be secondary. You can finish it after running just 1000K a year in preparation, and fail despite having 6000K under your belt. I think you only need to train as much as necessary to keep your confidence rock solid, so you can turn inward and meditate. After all, the last thing you need in the wee hours of the night, when you're shivering on the mountainside, is to start doubting yourself.

The only thing I asked Gabi – my wife and member of my support crew – was to remind me of my 2007 race if I started thinking about quitting. I asked her to remind me of the horrible, loathsome feeling I had the next morning. I had quit because it hurt and I didn't believe in myself. I didn't dare to keep going. Yet by the next day, when the pain started to subside, I couldn't understand what had happened. There was nothing wrong with me and I was even ahead of cut-off time. So, why didn't I push on? No. This time I'm not handing in my race-bib; they'll have to rip it off me. Never again will I walk around Sparta feeling ashamed, while the others are taking selfies by the statue of King Leonidas.

III

I got off the imaginary couch many times since 2008. I started every year saying that I would be at the next Spartathlon. But I probably didn't want it enough. I dreamed about Sparta's palm tree-lined finish and the spotlight. But I didn't want to put in the work. After all, the Spartathlon destroys you only to let you rise again. But was it still in me?

To my friends, I'm the runner. But the truth is that I only was a runner. Shame. Living with medals, plaques and race-bibs, memories of many past races; that was all once upon a time. The Olympian, who goes to his kids' school to talk about sports, just won't admit that he's not the runner he pretends to be.

The years came and went, it hurt here and there, but ultimately, I didn't put in the work needed for ultra running. I wasn't hungry and was content with an occasional marathon. Of course I still wanted to be the man who would do an extra loop on the afternoon run to hit 42K but I didn't want to work for it.

Four years ago though, we moved to Frankfurt, to a suburban neighborhood, next to pastures, woods, a river, and endless bike paths. If I couldn't make a comeback here, then I couldn't do it anywhere. This was a now or never moment, and this was where the 2019 Spartathlon started.

I started running, then stopped. Started again and got a bit further. I'd take two steps forward in my running, but only one step back. I managed a decent 100K then stopped again. It was such a mechanical, joyless process. My goal, the Spartathlon was too far away. And it was such a formidable target that all intermediate goals seemed pathetic. (I really know how to be my own worst enemy.)

Then something finally clicked last autumn. The excuses ran out and I went out running, then again, then again. I ran before dawn or late at night. If I was injured, I biked, sometimes arriving at work covered in mud.

Two people inspired me, through no fault of their own.

Ferenc Szekeres was an Olympic marathon runner back when I was still in diapers. And he is still running. He's not getting any younger and his knees are starting to go out on him, so he's cutting back on his distances. Still, he says that once his knees give out completely, he'll switch to biking.

Time is infinite, but our time isn't. Am I using mine wisely?

My other inspiration was Mark, a former track and field teammate from Rutgers University. Mark wasn't the fastest 800 runner but he never quit and barely slowed down. He's now (one of) the fastest men in the world in his age group.

What do these two guys have in common? They both love running.

For me, running was my first love and first loves are eternal.

So, in January, Gabi, who is a running coach in her spare time, sat down with me and took out a large sheet of paper. We then drew up a plan. We jotted down everything that I needed to do, set the major milestones and worked out the auxiliary stuff. Then I tacked this sheet up in the office to remind myself of my commitment.

IV

Despite its start line at the foot of the Acropolis, the beginning of the Spartathlon is not particularly pretty. Potholes, impatient drivers, and highways with subtle climbs mark the start. No, this wasn't the real Spartathlon. It is just a necessary evil, an objective circumstance that can't be changed, and it will eat your mental energy if you worry about it. Too many runners fail because they waste their mental energy. Gabi calls it the mental $100. You start your day with 100 mental dollars and your worries, about unchangeables, consume it. The bed in the hotel was too soft or the air on the flight was too dry? There were too many people at the aid stations so you had to get around a batch of cars, or the air at the refinery at Elefsfina was horrendous? Do you ever see András Lőw (21 Spartathlon finishes) worry about anything?

The refinery really is ugly. But like many things, it's part of a compromise deal. The throng of school kids cheering you on in Elefsfina more than offsets the refinery. As one Danish runner put it: these kids beat any other adrenaline rush.

My perfectly built, scientific Spartathlon race plan worked well until the end of the first marathon. That's where I made an almost fatal mistake, one that impacted my performance all the way to Sparta. I built a complex refreshment plan, calculating calories, carbs, proteins and salts. It worked perfectly in training. There was just one weakness: actually keeping to it. The plan relied on eating everything on schedule, whether I wanted it or not. But would I remember that? I sent food and drink in 22 care packages to various aid stations. The idea was that by the next package, everything I picked up previously should have been consumed.

Besides the food, I had my pills: food supplements, mostly salts. But there were amino acids, too, primarily BCAA. My quads are my weakest point and get tired first on long, monotonous runs, shortening my stride. But the BCAA pill seems to take care of this problem or at least buy me time. That's fine, of course, but I Googled the effect of BCAA and found a scientific paper which concluded that it had zero impact on ultramarathon performances. Great. (Stupid people should learn not to Google everything.) Still, my belief in BCAA hadn't been shaken, even if I now simply call it a placebo.

My pills – salt, calcium, magnesium, BCAA – were packed into smaller portions and sent along to the aid stations. Again, the idea was to consume everything from each package by the time I got to the next one. And this is where the applecart was upset. I was in a hurry and wanted to go through Megara (42K) too quickly. I forgot the pills! I grabbed the gels, the water bottle, then go, go, go!

Gabi spent months emphasizing that lingering too long at the aid stations was costly. The minutes went by for absolutely nothing. And I wanted to be a good student. I wanted to fly through Megara, showing that I was doing really well. But the truth was that I would have had time, all the time in the world. There was no point in rushing and I paid for this mistake with a panic attack.

It was hot, closing in on noon, and I was drenched in sweat. Without salt, it's over. This couldn't happen! This wasn't an objective circumstance to be tolerated; it was a blunder the Spartathlon would punish severely. My legs felt weak, I couldn't breathe. Like in the movie "Airplane," the "OKAY PANIC" sign came on. I turned inward. The amino acid might be a placebo, fine, but without salt in 32 C degrees (90F) I wouldn't be going far. But panic attacks aren't really helpful either. Why had I thought I wouldn't make a mistake? Why hadn't I seen this beforehand? I'd become overconfident.

Meanwhile, a British runner near me was slowing to a crawl. She was really struggling, then threw up. I turned around to see if I could help but she didn't even break a stride. To her, it was just an objective circumstance and not a source of panic. She kept on moving and passed me by.

No! There was no way that a runner who threw up could be mentally stronger than me. What had I been thinking?! That I was running in a 5K turkey chase?

OK, so I could beg other runners for salt, and the amino acid was supposed to be ineffective, anyway. I just needed to focus. Head down, face forward, run, walk, stop talking and move on. From here on, I needed to grab anything salty, even licking the bottom of a pretzel bag, if need be. I also had to slow down, not run the hills, and focus on the aid stations. No more mistakes!

V

Before the start, I slipped a piece of paper in my vest with a few reminders scribbled on it for a tired Balazs:

These are your best years – 45 is the new 30

The medal lasts forever, the pain is fleeting

Input = output. And you've done the work.

Your fate is in your own hands

You're not alone; your friends will be watching your transponder dot on the map all night long.

VI

András Lőw prompted me to do an honest comparison with my earlier self. Was this Spartathlon realistic or just a pipe dream?

The positives: I ran more this year than any other year, bar none. I ran 3000K (1860 miles) since Jan 1 and I kept raising the mileage. There were no missed weeks or big fluctuations like in the past. Instead, I ran five but more like six times a week. This is still important even if I accept my theory that ultra-running is an exercise in meditation. For me, this was the foundation of my self-confidence: that 45-year-old Balazs was stronger than his 34-year-old edition.

My understanding of nutrition has also improved. I tried a dozen new things this year and by August, I had a comprehensive refreshment schedule, something I didn't have in the past. To be honest, in my two Spartathlon finishes, my refreshments were ad hoc. I only focused on some variation but had no other concept behind it. In fact, I laughed at people who tried to be more scientific about their nutrition. But this year, my blood sugar level never fluctuated, even on the longest of runs, and that was already an improvement on my younger self.

The negatives: there were 11 mostly inactive years behind me. And even this year I didn't have any very long runs. I did 75K on my own and 120K in an Ultrabalaton relay in 10 segments. In fact the only ultra race I ran, (the Balaton Szupermaraton), I quit after 3 days.

Finally: I'm 45. I think this is the best age and I'm enjoying myself. And I have friends who really make me believe that this is the best age. A decade wiser, maybe I could look after my mental dollars better than earlier. But obviously I need more time to recover than during my Olympian years.

VII

Climbing up to the Corinth Canal (77K) wasn't easy. But that's a calculated hardship. A third of the race was over. (That's a stupid way of thinking. In terms of time, it was less than a quarter of the run, but I was happy to use the bigger number.) I was dehydrating. My urine was turning dark. Not good but I could still stop it. I was nearly to the aid station where I could get my pills from Gabi. And evening was coming, too.

I kept going and stuck to my mantra: Gotta move on, gotta move on!! (Talk about, talk about, talk about movin') But stop to look at the Corinth Canal, damn it, you're not a droid, after all! Take your time to think at the aid station! Don't waste time but do everything you need to do. Know what you want, keep repeating your list. No more mistakes, once you leave, you can't turn back.

At Corinth (80K) András was waiting for me. I instinctively asked what he was doing there, but deep down immediately knew that he was out of the race. And that felt like I had been punched in the stomach. Had the impossible just happened? Had an eternal truth, a fixed point in life been wiped out? A disturbance in the force … It's possible though that András' streak (19 straight Spartathlon finishes) was more important to me, to us, than to him. Because we feed from our role model's success and because we share our friends' pain and joy ….

Cal Ripken was a baseball player, not a runner, but he started in over 2600 consecutive games in over 18 years. That record will never be broken. Towards the end of the 1998 season, Ripken chose to sit out a game so the streak wouldn't pressure him anymore and so he could finish it on his own terms. Then the next day, he played again and the world didn't end. András: I hope that you keep finding joy in the Spartathlon.

VIII

I was afraid of Corinth. It was a dangerous check point. There were chairs, mattresses, and shade everywhere. And for hours, all I wanted was to reach this point. But I could only stay for a minute or two. A high five and I was out there again in the scorching sun.

My pills weren't in the Corinth package, either. Damn it! But Gabi replenished me from András' stock. I even got some placebo. I just needed to screw my head on straight. You OK, I asked? Totally. I had everything I needed so I only had to pull myself together. I had an hour's lead on the cut-off time and my legs were fine, said I. And now the best part was coming up; the orange groves, the vineyards, the tiny villages. Finally, the real Spartathlon was getting underway.

To the left, vineyards, and the smell of fresh must. Idyllic. Kids on bikes, farms, quiet. I wasn't really well but was getting better. It took a while to get over the panic that hit me after the Megara aid station. I was more dehydrated more than I had hoped. But it was early evening and ultimately, nothing was wrong. András was also waiting for me in Ancient Corinth (93K). He had joined my support crew of Gabi and Bogi, a family friend who was visiting from Sydney. His wretched luck became my good fortune. What a contradiction.

They fed me tzatziki then threw me out of the check point. (You have anything left to do here? You could do this on the road ....) But, I wasn't done. I stopped around the next corner, threw out my trash, packed up the fresh stuff, washed my hands, and got my gear in order. OK, go! I don't know how many sports gels I ate but I can run forever on plastic food. Perhaps it's my stomach that scientists are looking for: I can turn plastic garbage into bio compost.

IX

The Spartathlon also suffers from a big contradiction: its selection process. The last time I ran, anybody who qualified got to run. In the interim the world changed. The cost of popularity is that they have to be selective. This course can't handle more than 400 runners, or to be more precise, the support crew and cars of the 400. But the qualification system favors the fast runners who automatically qualify and get to skip the lottery. This skews the process towards the elite. And seriously, how is a sub 8-hour 100K a relevant quality? After a 100K, you're home for dinner and even have time to watch a film. How is that going to help you at dawn, when you're staggering along the highway?

The problem is that such a qualification system – in my opinion – threatens the innocence of the race. It has become more and more popular, so it is tougher to get in. The faster runners will get to take up more spots and fewer will be left for the ordinary ultra-runners.

The Spartathlon is not an elite race. Its current legends are not particularly fast runners. It is the average runners who made this race what it is now. And I hope it can stay open to ordinary people.

X

Zevgolatio (102K) is one of the magical spots in the race, with the applauding priest, the cute town square, and the kids lining up for autographs. Only once before had kids ever swarmed me, asking for autographs. That was in 1998 after the European Championships in athletics. I had just run a national record on the 800m and for a brief moment, I was a star. I promised to give everyone an autograph, even if I had to stay all night. I'm still keeping that promise and wouldn't turn away any of those kids, even if I missed the cut-off time. Those kids will be the ones keeping the Spartathlon going in a few years' time so if we're not doing something for them, then the Spartathlon really is just a selfish act.

Villages like this follow one after the other: Nemea, Malandreni, Lyrkia, Kaparelli, and Nestani are pearls in the night, shunned by main roads. And there's a good chance that the Spartathlon is also their biggest night of the year.

XI

Running up the Nemea valley, I gained a bit of strength gaining on the cut-off times. After every mile that I walked, I felt refreshed and able to run once again. Only my quads ached. (Where's the placebo!?)

Around Nemea (123K), the bodies started to appear. In chairs, on mattresses. A few would get up but most would end up on the bus to Sparta that collected people who ran out of time. In an average year, only half of the starters finish. Poor Bogi, my support crew was doing her first ultra. How this must have looked!

There were only few people around me by now. The field was stretched out and night had fallen. Steven, an American runner, asked where we were. At 136K, I said. No, in miles, please. Umm … er … damn it … umm, yes! 85! Nice! I can still do math, so my brain is functioning.

In the distance, I could already see the mountain that we were about to climb. It didn't appear too high. So, why do we all dread it? I was almost glad about the climb. I was tired and had an excuse to walk. There's no point in running up a hill and by the time we reach the other side, the running muscles will feel rested. At the check points Gabi kept feeding me coffee and soup while András kept filling my water bottles. I was slowing but there was nothing wrong and I was increasing my lead on the cut-off times.

Going up the mountain, I kept passing people and even the trail didn't scare me. This wasn't right. I'd been dreading this climb for six months. Coming down didn't feel all that great but it was a relief. I descended into the Tripoli basin which meant I'd covered two-thirds of the distance. Comparatively few people quit beyond this point. It was past 3 am. And now had hours to run the flats in the cool night.

XII

After Sagkas (162K) a dog started to run with me. He was behind me but once I started walking, he passed me, signaling that this was not walking event. Then another runner went past me, and dog went on with him. Fine, go, you faithless! Run your own race. When I got to the next check point, the dog was being given a drink. His runner hadn't waited for him, so he joined me again. Disloyal bastard!

It was getting cold. My crew was tired. Bogi was jetlagged and kept wanting to dress me in sweats at every check point. András was wearing Gabi's size S sweatshirt. None of us were having fun at that moment.

I ran more during the night than in any previous Spartathlon. I found extra energy in hidden compartments and ran segments that gave me trouble in the past. But the bubble burst at dawn. As it got light, I panicked and forgot the number one rule: that you merely have to get to the next aid station and not Sparta.

It hit me that in a few hours, it would be over 30 C degrees again. I freaked out at the thought that there were still 10 hours to go and the pavement would soon be boiling again. My legs simply stopped from the shock. It never got truly cold overnight, so I stayed in my daytime gear. But I was still sweating.

XIII

Stick with Béla, a Hungarian runner who just passed me, said Gabi. Stick with him. Finally! Proof that she's trying to murder me. But fine, let me give it a go. At this pace, my finish time will start with 33 hours. We passed Tegea (195K), turned onto the main road and I started to push the climb, like the mountain pass overnight. I was making progress but running on empty.

I slowed down and Béla left me behind. I got sleepy again. That's impossible, nobody's sleepy at 9:30 in the morning. My eyes closed. No! Not here! You'll die! There are 18-wheelers whizzing by. I started walking with my eyes closed. I just had to get to the next aid station. Alive, preferably. I asked for coffee. They only had instant. How many spoonfuls? All them! burned my mouth. Damn it! The same place as last time! I pulled myself together and seemed to be holding my lead on the cut-offs. As I approached the monument (223K) I came alive and started running. Mile after mile. Easy. Right turn and food. Wow! Tuna! I packed up my stuff and moved on. My strength was back. Go, go, go! Gabi, Bogi and András have a routine by now. Water bottle out, ice water in, gels, drink in, then go!

On the last big hill, I lost power again. No problem, that's happened before. A bit of walking, then I'll be OK.

XIV

Jesus, where are we going? Left turn off the main road. I've never been here before. But there are like 15 yellow arrows. What's happening? Erika, a Hungarian runner who kept me company last night, passes by. I'm not well and everything around me is strange. My body is burning up. It's much hotter than yesterday. I can't run. Everything is dry, I'm not sweating anymore. But that's impossible. I'm eating the salts like it's free. But the salty water is just sitting in my stomach. I try to run the downhills but it's no use; my knees buckle. The heat radiating off the pavement is literally burning my skin. Don't panic! I have plenty of time but unless I can cool down I'm in trouble. I'm not going to finish in less than 34 hours, but I should make it in under 35! Only I need to move ….

My water bottle was full of ice. I kept spraying myself but after a few minutes, I was dry again. I realized that I was completely dehydrated, and unable to sweat or to run. But I was still moving though very slowly. I just had to keep going! There was no need to run but stopping was out of the question. I timed my pace. 11 minutes per kilometer. It didn't matter, as long as I was moving.

I got to the gas station (236K). András inadvertently said that it took too long. I didn't want to worry them. The last thing I needed was Gabi freaking out. I filled my vest, drenched myself, got the ice, and took off. Only 10K! Less than two hours, if I kept moving. I still wasn't sweating but kept cooling myself with ice and water. There was more shade now and I took the longer arc on curves to help me avoid the sun for a few extra seconds. Then I ate one more gel as though it would do any good. 90 minutes to the finish, 85, 82 ... I was burning but moving. Kriszta, another Hungarian, passed me. She slowed down to cheer me up. Thanks! Then Kladas (241K) and the Evrotas (244K). Andrei Nana from the U.S. caught up to me. He's got number 7! Well done, congrats. Everything was OK, I was just about there, I'll have managed to get my third finish.

XV

After the first turn in Sparta, I started to jog again. Applause came from every balcony, store, and street corner. Kids on bikes met me; adults patted me on the shoulder. There's love and respect everywhere. I came to this race for these few minutes. Those moments will feed me for years to come. I pulled my hat down onto my face and swallowed my tears. I did it! Not just the 246K. But the 45 year old Balazs beat his younger edition. I never doubted myself while the younger versions were never sure until the finish line. I'm really running again and this time I won't quit.

A hundred meters, 50, 25. And a crowd like I had never seen here before. Gabi got the first hug but I was not great company, I was so full of emotion. At the statue of Leonidas, George, like always, stepped behind me, ready to grab me if I struggled up the stairs. But I didn't need him this time. I lay my head down in front of the statue for just a few brief moments. Everything was quiet and I relived this journey. The plaque and the wreath are just props. The moment with the statue, with my back to the crowd, is the real one. When nobody's watching my face, when it's just me. When I didn't yet need to shake hands and smile for the camera. I did it!

XVI

I wrote the end of this report in my head after Voutianoi (236K), on the scorching pavement. This race has been a central part of my life since 2005. That's a third of my life. Even during the years I sat on the couch, I dreamed of this day. Now, the cycle has ended. I fulfilled a decade-long dream so it's time to let go and close the chapter. And how else do you say good bye to a king than with a victory?

But I didn't manage to open the laptop on the day of the race so I never got this ending down on paper. And by the time I typed it up, it didn't sound honest.

As Eiolf Eivind of Norway said on Sunday, puzzled by me saying never again: if it wasn't terribly hard, it wouldn't be the Spartathlon. And then there would be no point, either.

I can't escape this race. It's an eternal love affair. It's the sort of love you want to throw the china at, but then get mad when they don't chat you up on Messenger. It's a love affair you're pissed at for pushing you to the wall, but deep down you know it's only to get the best out of you.

Godspeed Leonidas, I'm afraid we'll meet again.

There's a Poem in this Run

amy mower

There's a poem in this run
if only I can find it
hidden
(perhaps)
between my rain slicker
and running shirt
or maybe
in the pouch
next to my water bottle
that mostly holds food
but sometimes holds poems

The poetry is coalescing
on the skin on my face
as the tiny droplets
that weren't even supposed
to be falling
come together and
run in rivulets
down my cheeks

The poetry
of running blind
my glasses held gently
in my soaking wet gloves,
too rain-spattered to be of use
In this gentle dark misty blur
It is just me and
the run
and the poem
that is starting to form

Salt Flats 100
walter handloser

"In the central portion of the great North American Continent there lies an arid and repulsive desert, which for many a long year served as a barrier against the advance of civilisation. From the Sierra Nevada to Nebraska, and from the Yellowstone River in the north to the Colorado upon the south, is a region of desolation and silence. [...] It comprises snow-capped and lofty mountains, and dark and gloomy valleys. There are swift-flowing rivers which dash through jagged cañons; and there are enormous plains, which in winter are white with snow, and in summer are grey with the saline alkali dust. They all preserve, however, the common characteristics of barrenness, inhospitality, and misery." -Sir Arthur Conan Doyle, "A Study in Scarlet"

Jesus, Doyle, chill already. The race wasn't THAT bad.

By a show of hands, how many of you are familiar with the Bonneville Salt Flats? Really? That many? Ok, for those of you who didn't raise your hand, a primer:

The Bonneville Salt Flats are exactly as advertised: they're salt, and they're flat. And they're huge. Nearly 110 miles on the long axis and 40 on the short, the flats dwarf their neighbor, the Great Salt Lake. Together, they comprise the seasonal remnants of the prehistoric Lake Bonneville. The Flats still flood every winter, turning the salt into a shallow, warm lake which, despite being hundreds of square miles, mostly doesn't get more than a few inches deep. Interstate 80 crosses the flats east-to-west across the middle like a belt, and for that time runs so straight they have signposts to calibrate speedometers.

Now when I say the Salt Flats are flat, I mean really, really flat. I called C&O Canal flat, but it has nothing, NOTHING on the Salt Flats. C&O is runner flat. Bonneville is world's fastest rocket car flat. They are so flat for so long that objects literally disappear over their horizon. As you drive west across the flats from SLC, a gas station seems to magically appear, lifting itself up above the horizon line as you approach.

Normally the Salt Flats 100 starts on these same flats, in the staging area where trucks pull up hauling rocket cars and super-powered motorcycles for testing on the flats. The runners start directly out onto the salt to the northeast, heading for a distant "island" 20 miles out. "The Islands" is the collective name given to the mountains that puncture the salt flats in places. They'd have been real islands in the Pleistocene days of Lake Bonneville. Now they're just irregular land features in the otherwise pure, unbroken white of the salt.

Sadly, with the long, wet winter that's held a grip on the west, the flats are still flooded, turning the staging area into a four-mile-long paved isthmus in a huge, shallow lake. Which means the normal 20-mile run across the salt has to be rerouted. The race has an alternate course for these years: rather than out, you run in along the road for four miles, then turn north where the road meets the edge of the salt flats, skirting the islands the entire time. Impressively, the race manages to re-use very little course even in the alternate version. The alternate has the four-mile starting isthmus and a small bit of connective trail perhaps totaling three extra miles. Aside from that, this is a real single-loop course.

With the preliminaries out of the way, I'll say that my own race experience was … well, let's just say I came into this race exhausted and not really stoked on being there. That's bound to happen with this many races in a year. You can't be up for all of them. Some of them are bound to just be filling a space in the roster. This is no negative against the race, just a reflection on the fact that your motivation doesn't always track with your goals. Sometimes the motivation is there; other times it's not but you have a thing to do and you do it anyway.

Motivation is transient. Rely on it, and you'll fail when you need it most.

This week, I had a job: complete the race. That was pretty much it. Salt Flats has no special sub-24 buckle, no weird or otherwise unique placement awards. It's just an old fashioned race across the desert. There was no pressure to be amazing, and so I wasn't even going to try. I was glad that Jackie was here and had a goal she was after. Looking through the entrants' CVs on UltraSignup, it seemed within reason that she could win the women's 50k race. I went in more stoked on that possibility than in anything I was going to do. The 50k is an out-and-back on the alternate course, going out to the second aid station and back. The 50 miler is a lollipop loop of part of the 100-miler course. Since 50k and 50 mile people start at the same time as the 100-milers, the start of the race is a crowded, social thing, and for the first dozen or so miles there's constant passing.

I'm going to skip over a lot of the first 50 miles. It's not that they're terrible, it's that they can be summed up rather easily: Trail running along well-behaved trails along the base of foothill-sized mountains. The views from the south side of the islands are a seemingly unbroken white plain ringed by extremely distant mountains. Interstate 80 runs through the center of the view as a distant dark line. There's one major climb in the first half, but otherwise the miles go by largely without incident.

I've mentioned before that one of the "hidden" difficulties of a trail race is the number of aid stations. If you were to categorize the non-elevation-related difficulty factor of a race, it would probably be something like (technicality) times (weather) divided by (support), where support is the number of aid stations and weather is some combination of heat and exposure, while technicality encompasses all aspects of footing. A well-supported hundred will have something like 20 aid stations, or one every five-ish miles. Old Dominion has a shocking 25, while San Diego has a relatively paltry 15. Salt Flats has 14 manned aid stations and near total exposure. There is not a single shadow to be had during the entire day on the trail. As if that weren't enough, the aid stations aren't evenly spaced, with sometimes as much as 11 miles between manned stations, and only hand-pumpable water buckets to get you through the worst of them. This is all to say that Salt Flats gains a lot of its difficulty in the psychological toll of long aid station breaks and extremely long sight lines that make it seem like hours pass without any noticeable change.

And by almost 50 miles in, this had begun to take its toll. One of the final straws, for me at least, had been the mud flats. The mud flats are a ten-mile section of course between 40 and 50 that only the hundred-milers get to experience. Picture running across a soft, dry lake bed overlooked by a snow-capped mountain. Now do that for two straight hours. The ground in the mud flats had just dried out the day before, so it was still soft. Runners had to follow a pair of tire tracks, running heel-to-toe to stay in the hard packed ground left by the weight of the car. Occasionally that section would become rough and you'd have to switch to the other track, then back again when the new track had issues. All the while, the mountain, which I found out later was the 10700' Pilot Peak, seemed to loom overhead, huge and unchanging.

To cap the whole mess off, you can see almost the entirety of the ten-mile section from only a few miles in. Your fellow runners in front of and behind you look like tiny, unmoving dots against the horizon. If there are runners behind you, it can be a real struggle not to feel chased and pick up your pace. I made a conscious decision not to look backward the entire time. Of course, that long sight line means that the view forward has its own issues: the aid station (Hastings Junction) comes into view more than an hour before you reach it, almost so small it could be missed against the desert scrub backdrop. In actuality, the station is a huge collection of three or four sturdy tents, several parked cars, and a bright red portable toilet, all of which blend at that extreme distance to a handful of brightly colored specks at the base of a distant hill.

Coming out of that section, I was done. I mean, I was still moving, and I wasn't that bad off physically. But I was mentally fried. One of the two distant runner dots that had been in front of me had stopped at this aid station, looking like the guy who's about to turn in a zombie flick, and at least on the inside I could relate. I'm not sure if he ended up continuing the race, and right about then I could sympathize with the decision.

I call out this particular point not only as a race low, but as the place where the race kind of turned around for me. Because about two or three miles outside of Hastings Junction, I caught the next person up, Kilian Korth. At that point, I had been running in close sight of him for a while, and our pace was so nearly equal that, if left alone, we might have cruised along a few hundred yards from one another the whole race. At that point, though, I needed some company, and so I kicked it up to a full run for a while to catch up. Sometimes you've just got to take a chance that your fellow runner isn't an asshole. 99% of the time, with ultrarunning, that's true, and you can make an instant trail friend. Luckily, this time, I got all that and more.

I've said this previously, and I don't think it can be emphasized enough: find your reason to continue wherever you can. For me, in this race, that reason became Kilian. Kilian is a younger runner as ultrarunners go, still in his early 20's. He came to the sport through his older brother, who he clearly has a lot of admiration for. He was in Salt Flats running his second hundred, and he was out for revenge. His previous 100 had taken him 31 hours, and it was a time he wasn't happy with. His goal here was to come back from that first finish and try for his first sub-24. And as soon as I learned that, I had my reason to keep moving forward.

Kilian turned out to be nearly the perfect trail companion. Our pace was near identical, we had extremely similar interests, and we both enjoyed a good argument. Fueled by that, we spent the next ten hours in nearly constant conversation. Kilian was running a strong race, but his stomach was holding him back, and digestive issues were leading to frequent stops. Still, I knew that despite that, both of us would be faster together than apart. So we kept with it for the rest of the night, steadily plugging our way through the final 45 miles of the race. I've never spent so much time in a race with the same fellow runner, and I've also never enjoyed the resulting conversation quite so much. Despite the stops, we kept a solid 12 minute pace while moving, and the sub 24 seemed more and more inevitable.

The final half of the race is the harder half, having bigger and more frequent climbs, including a seemingly interminable seven-miler leading to the final important aid station at mile 90. Coming down the far side of that hill, I don't think I've ever looked behind me quite so often. I'm not one to get caught up in competition, but sometimes a trailing headlamp can be a great gut check as to whether you're really doing as well as you think. It's a bit of context, if you will. All evening, we had been seeing headlamps at the edge of visibility, but with the massive sight lines this race affords, that could mean they were fifteen minutes or fifteen miles behind us. Still, their presence there egged us on, and when we came to the base of the final downhill and just had the long, straight, flat five final miles of paved road ahead, I could look behind us and see the first headlamps just cresting the hill almost five miles back. That's when I knew we were safe.

We ran the final few miles in at our own pace, and Kilian came in right around 21:29, knocking more than 10 hours off his previous fastest 100. We came in third and fourth male, with the overall winner being the amazing Steph Whitmore , who had taken the first women's overall win in the race's nine-year history. My own bit of good news came in shortly after I had finished: Jackie had in fact won the women's 50k division.

What Now

karen fennie

What will we do now
With most of the distractions removed
When we become reacquainted with the voice inside
And the voices of others around us

Maybe it will be like the coming of spring when the early morning
quiet is gradually disturbed
And there is more song in the air
What songs will we sing?

The roads are quieter already
More discover the outdoors and the gift that has been around them
all this time
We have wandered for too long too far away from this grace that
sustains us
The everyday miracle of the trees and the clouds and the rain and
the sun

Clearly I am on my soapbox now
But there is much to learn in this season of birth
The slow unfolding of the leaves and all manner of life being
pulled up through the soil by the inexorable sun

This could be a second chance is what I'm thinking
If we can open our hearts with the same joy a daffodil greets the
sun
And abide the same brave faith the trees display
Though they know eventually
They will lose
Everything

About the Authors

Shamus Babcock

Shamus Babcock (aka Sean Gavor) is an ultra-pedestrian, classically trained scientist, gardener, and USPS city letter carrier who writes about his race experiences from his location in Central New Jersey. He has competed in foot racing events ranging from 200 meters to 500 kilometers and has also served as race crew duties for other runners in multi-day running events. He is the creator of the popular Path to Victory jogging route, can grow scorpion peppers from seed, and has a beer mile time of 7 minutes 19 seconds.

Brian Burk

Brian is presently a Mechanical Skills Instructor with a fortune 100 company living and working out of North Carolina and Virginia. Prior to his present position, he retired from the United States Air Force after serving as a Senior Noncommissioned Officer (SMSgt). During a 20-year military career, he served state side, and tours overseas including a remote tour to Thule, Greenland and a combat tour in Northern Iraq. He originally hails from Erie, PA. Not a natural runner, Brian found his passion for running in his 30s. Since then his running career has seen him complete race distances from 5k to 100-miles in length. Likewise, writing came on late. Brian could tell a gripping story but found it hard to get it onto paper. "Unfinished" is his third book. His other works include, "Running to Leadville", his first novel and "26.2 Tips to run your best MARATHON". He has also been published in national running publications, running theme blogs and his blog at http://briansrunningadventures.com. Follow Brian on Twitter and Instagram @cledawgs or like his Facebook page

Dr. Lisa Butler

Dr. Butler considers herself a Creative trapped in an analytical mind. Her day job involves science, analysis, and a wealth of tasks that leave little time for creativity. Her creative spirit awakens when she runs and bikes. With body and brain off leash as she runs alone through the mountains of Colorado, she can hear the universe whispering poetry. When not running, she enjoys creating pretty messes through many forms of art including painting and fiber art.

She began writing poetry at about age 10 and running at age 14. Some 4 + decades later, both are still a part what makes her heart beat. They are the meditation that remind her that the essence of everything is love. She does her best to carry that into her work as a physician practicing the art of medicine.

As an ultrarunner for over 25 years, she has had the joy of running in many parts of the country and a few other far flung places. Her muse is the rhythm of breathing when the pace and place have outdistanced stress.

Gary Cantrell (aka Lazarus Lake)

Gary Cantrell writes the "View From the Open Road" column. Gary has written for Ultrarunning more or less continuously since his column "From the South" first appeared in Volume 1, Number 1 back in May of 1981. He is perhaps most well-known as the founder of the Barkley, a trail race in eastern Tennessee. (Although some would comment that it isn't really a race, and others would add that those aren't really trails). He is also the founder of the Strolling Jim 40 Mile and periodically organizes a 314-mile run across Tennessee the Vol State Road Race. He is currently the race director of the Backyard Ultra. In the real world he works as an accountant.

Mary Ann Clute

Mary Ann Clute started writing as a child. She started running over 40 years ago while she was getting her Masters in Social Work. Her husband then began running, as well. She ran through two pregnancies and child rearing while working many social work jobs. She ran and ran until she fell in love with ultramarathons and multi day races. She ran and wrote poems throughout her PhD program. She ran to stay more balanced than unbalanced in her years as a social work educator and hospice bereavement counselor. She runs now in retirement and finds a sense of calm and creativity whether she is on the road or trail.

Kimberly Durst

Kim Durst is a 36 year-old single mom, nurse, with a bachelor's degree in religion from Hiram where she focused on Buddhism. She's been running since the age of 13, and became interested in multi-day running when she and her sister hatched a plan to backpack the railroad tracks when they were 17 to see how far they could get. She is an introvert and writes poetry and stories while she runs. She says "I use humor in writing because I have poor social skills ... Running makes me feel alive and aware of myself."

Scotty Louise Eckert

Scotty was born in Brownsville, Texas on September 25, 1946 with a thick black head of hair. At 4 years old she and her family moved to Long Island, NY where she developed her love of the woods. She grew up during the times of assassinations, JFK, MLK and RFK, and the Vietnam War which had a huge impact on who she is today. She worked with autistic children for many years and then worked in animal rescue. She and her husband, John, have three children and two grandchildren. Scotty's family has always been the most important thing in her life.

John Ehntholt

John describes himself as a "small town country boy". He was a sprinter in high school and found his way back to running afterwards. He started running after retiring from competitive Martial Arts in 2002 ... worked his way up to marathon distance in 2005 and then onto Ultra Marathons in 2008. *5k PR: 17:33 *Marathon PR: 2:48 *50k PR: 3:33 *50 Mile PR: 6:23 100 Mile PR: 17:33:20   He finds it funny that his 5k and 100 Mile PR's are both 17:33 and wonders if others find the same or close to theirs as well. A welder by trade, he loves the mountains for their challenge and beauty. He is a big fan of baked goods and hates being serious.

Karen Fennie

Karen ran a bunch of marathons starting in 1996. Karen's first ultra was accidental. A friend said 'you can always turn around and come back' . This was around 2005 or 2006. But she didn't turn around and after completing a 50k she wondered if she could run 50 miles. And after running 50 miles she wondered if she could run 100. She ran her first 100 in 2008 and has run a bunch more 100's, 50's and 50k's since then. She lives in upstate NY, works at a University, putters in flower and veggie gardens and fosters kitties sometimes. She has been a race director in the past, volunteers at races still, crews friends at ultras and after cleaning the muddy feet of a friend who had just finished a 100 miler, was told, 'you're just like Jesus washing the feet. Ultra Jesus'. She has no idea of how many miles she's run though could come up with a guess if she looked through all the old school logs. She doesn't have a Garmin.

Adrian Gentry

Adrian is a trail runner and through hiker, born in the UK but now residing in sunny Ontario. A fan of unsupported point to point hikes he grew up running the North Downs Way in England and now lives just a few miles from the Bruce Trail trial head in Niagara.

Bill Gentry

Bill Gentry has covered more than 100,000 miles since he started running in 1976. He ran his first ultramarathon in 1991 and thinks that life imitates ultras.

William Hafferty

Billy is probably still hanging out of the passenger side of his best friend's ride trying to holler at you

Walter Handloser

Walter Handloser is an ultra-runner who got there the hard way. After spending most of his life obese, he got his life together, shaped up, lost 105 lbs, and started a semi healthy running addiction right around his 30th birthday. 25 marathons and 91 ultra-marathons later, he's still just as addicted as the day he started. In 2019 he set out to take the record for the most 100+ mile races run in a year.

Bob Hearn

Bob Hearn has run more than 160 marathons and ultras, including Badwater, two Western States, and three Spartathlons. Known for his analytical approach to race planning and pacing, Bob was the first American over 50 to break the 150-mile barrier in 24 hours. He holds several age-group American records for ultra distances, from 100 miles to 48 hours, and has twice won the naked division of the Burning Man 50K. Earlier in life, he co-wrote the classic Macintosh program ClarisWorks. He holds a Ph.D. in computer science from MIT, and is co-author of the book "Games, Puzzles, and Computation". He currently serves on the board of the Gathering 4 Gardner, an organization promoting the playful exchange of ideas and critical thinking in recreational math, magic, science, literature, and puzzles. Bob lives with his wife Liz (the real runner of the family), their cat Lily, and his extensive mechanical puzzle collection in Portola Valley, California.

Balazs Koranyi

Balazs Koranyi started off as a sprinter and made it to two Olympic semi-finals in the 800 meters before wanting to do something completely different. So he naturally picked up ultramarathoning and went from the half mile to a 100K in one go. On the day-job, he writes about European monetary policy for a wire service in Frankfurt and on the evening shifts he builds Lego with his twin boys or stars in their cringeworthy TikToks.

Bob Lantz

Bob Lantz is a 66 year old father of 6. A veteran of the USMC and a retired Steam Boiler Operator, he has been running for most of his life. He has run about 30 marathons (Boston twice) with a marathon personal best of 3:17, and about 40 ultras, with the longest being 35 miles. In addition to running, he kayaks and bikes. He lives in the rural mountains along the Susquehanna river in Northeast Pennsylvania.

Patrick McHenry

Pat McHenry has been many things over the course of his nearly sixty years on this planet: student, USAF Airman, software engineer, husband of one, father of two, downhill skier, picker of stocks, award-winning homebrewer and certified judge of beers, snowmobiler, weightlifter, runner, writer of things never published, sinner, and saint. Right now he might best be described as a pedestrian musician who sometimes participates in very long pedestrian races – "but that's just right now."

Amy Mower

Amy Mower is a recovering sloth, alcoholic, smoker and food addict. Her current addiction is running, which she generally does daily at a time her friend Deb describes as "in the middle of the fucking night". She runs to find joy and do battle with demons. Her other hobbies include knitting, baking and writing. She is married to Benjamin ("BJ") Timoner who is her biggest supporter and an ultra pedestrian in his own right, having completed 2 transcons.

Bonnie Muetterties

Bonnie has been a runner for 33 years. She started out doing triathlons. With 5 children it became too time consuming. Running, however, was fast, flexible, and convenient. She wanted to run a race at every distance to see where her strengths were. She found that the longer she ran, the more success she had. It was the sport she enjoyed the most as well. Running feeds her body, soul and spirit and she feel so blessed to continue this passion.

Fred Murolo

Fred Murolo has run every day for over 38 years. Although not possessing elite talent or speed, he has completed forty 100 milers and 10 multiday races. Most of all, he enjoys the exquisite feeling of the daily run. He lives and works in Connecticut with his wife.

Alene Nitzky

Alene Nitzky started running in 1984 and has been running ultras since 1991. She lives in Fort Collins, Colorado with her husband and their two Australian Shepherds.

George Sanders

After a less than auspicious high school career, George returned to running in 1968 and discovered he was no longer a back of the pack runner. After moving from Illinois to Connecticut he discovered road racing, which inevitably led to testing the marathon waters at Boston. While having moderate success at the marathon distance with an eventual PB of 2:54, his real love was the track and short road races. After 45 years, with the inevitable slow down due to aging, and the lack of competition in his age group, he looked for something new to renew his enjoyment of running and racing. He decided to check out ultra marathons, something completely different. As the cliché has it, the rest is history. He has raced ultras on the road, the track, and trails, but mostly has embraced fixed time races.

Dani Seiss

Dani Seiss works for a magazine by day for which she takes and edits photos, produces photo shoots, and writes on occasion. On weekends and in the evenings she runs, gardens, writes, plays, makes art and music and seeks adventure with her husband, Curt and dog Miko. She has been running long races since 2008, but has been running long distances in the mountains since she her teens.

Dallas Smith

Dallas Smith is Professor Emeritus at Tennessee Tech University where he taught engineering. After leaving academic life he took up full-time running and writing. He holds several dozen single-age running records in Tennessee, ranging over a spectrum of distances from 5k to marathon. He has gained first-place in his age group at dozens of marathons, including the Chicago Marathon and the New York City Marathon. He has completed Ironman triathlons and 100-mile ultramarathons. Three times he has finished the 314-mile foot race known as The Last Annual Vol State Road Race. His books, Falling Forward (2004), Going Down Slow (2011), and Bench of Despair (2016), deal with the adventure aspects of endurance. He lives in Cookeville, Tennessee with his wife Jo Ann. He can be reached on Facebook or on Twitter @smithbend or by email at: dallassmith@charter.net.